SNOWDONIA

NATIONAL PARK GUIDE NUMBER 2

ISSUED FOR THE

NATIONAL PARKS COMMISSION

LONDON

HER MAJESTY'S STATIONERY OFFICE

1958: *Reprinted* 1960

This guide-book was prepared by the Snowdonia Park Joint Advisory Committee under the editorship of Edmund Vale (who also takes responsibility for all those parts of the text not ascribed to another author).

CONTENTS

A Topographical Description of the Park

ILLUSTRATIONS

PLATES

[1] Inscriptions (after V. E. Nash-Williams): (*a*) CANTIORI(x) HIC JACIT (v)ENEDOTIS CIVE(s) FUIT (c)ONSOBRINO(s) MA(g)LIT MAGISTRATI. *Cantorix lies here. He was a citizen of Venedos (and) cousin of Maglos the Magistrate.* 'Venedos' is the ancient form of 'Gwynedd'. (*b*) The *Chi-Rho* symbol (for Christos), then—CARAUSIUS HIC JACIT IN HOC CONGERIES LAPIDUM. *Carausius lies here in this heap of stones.* Both fifth-sixth century, the former clearly indicating that some relic of Roman administration still remained in force in this corner of the old Empire.

Illustrations

MAPS

ACKNOWLEDGMENT

I would like to express my thanks to the staffs of the Snowdonia National Park Joint Advisory Committee and the National Parks Commission for much help and courtesy during the preparation of this Guide. I owe a particular dept of gratitude to the authors of the five special articles which bear their names. My thanks are also due to Professor R. Alun Roberts for reading the proof sheets; to Mr. W. J. Hemp, whose unique knowledge of the archaeology of Wales was always available, and to Mr. Colin Gresham; to Dr. Elfyn Hughes of the Nature Conservancy; to Mr. H. J. D. Tetley, of the National Trust; to Mr. D. Miller for allowing me to use two of his exceptionally fine collection of photographs of British alpine flora (Plate II), and to that admirable Nature-taught naturalist, Mr. Evan Roberts, Warden of the Nature Reserves within the National Park.

The Publishers wish to acknowledge their indebtedness to the photographers whose work is reproduced in the plates named below:

Baxter's Studios, Llandudno IV b; K. R. Davidson I (frontispiece), VIII, X b, XI b; J. R. Edwards X a, XIII a; J. C. Flemons XVII b; W. W. Harris III a, XIII b; Prof. H. R. Hewer III b; A. L. Hutton XV; Ronald Thompson IX, XI a, XIV b, XVI a and b; Valentine, Dundee XIV a; Crown Copyright IV a, V a, b and c, VI, VII a and b, XII a and b, XVII a.

The cover illustration is of 'Bethgelert Bridge' and is taken from a 19th century engraving in the Hulton Picture Library.

THE EDITOR

A NATIONAL PARK

THE word *park* is an old one. It meant, in the first instance, a fenced enclosure in which the lord of a manor preserved wild game which he had the sole right of hunting for his own pleasure. National Parks in North America and Africa were also first instituted for the preservation of the native fauna. But the aim was in reverse—it was to save the animals from extinction and to give not one person but the general public an opportunity of observing their natural way of life when unmolested (except under very restricted conditions) by the sportsman.

In Britain, the idea of protection has been greatly extended to embrace the landscape itself. Our climate—about which we complain so much—and our geological heritage—about which the average man hardly bothers his head—has given us a countryside which, for variety and beauty, is unique in all the world. But it is a birthright whose singular virtues (expressed inadequately by the term 'amenities') have lately been threatened by piecemeal decimation. To prevent this happening, a concentrated effort has been made by public-spirited people to save some of the best unspoilt areas by designating them National Parks. Thus, the old word *park* has moved so far from its original meaning of a hunter's preserve as to stand for what is virtually a human sanctuary.

The Snowdonia National Park covers an area that very nearly coincides with the ancient realm of Gwynedd, whose ruler, by the middle of the 13th century, was acknowledged the most powerful of all the heads of native dynasties and could style himself Prince of Wales. This was doubtless due in great measure to the physical nature of the country where the highest and roughest mountains were concentrated, making a natural fortress, successfully held against competitor powers of the same nation, against the Norman settlers in the March lands, and against all the might of the English crown until the war waged by Edward I in 1282.

Those same mountains, which for so long were military assets when kingdom was divided against kingdom, have now reversed their role to become assets of peace. And what, it may be asked, are these assets of peace? Can one follow up the analogy in terms of valuation? The answer is an affirmative in two kinds, spiritual and physical, and may be summarised as follows.

On the spiritual side there is, first and foremost, the power of environment exercised by natural beauty—endless miles of it, where roads follow through wooded valleys watered by clear, rushing rivers, and through high mountain passes. Or, again, where paths and ancient trackways on open moorland lead away from the routes of wheeled vehicles up into the heart of the hills, where Nature has pursued the long course of evolution to no other human accompaniment but that of the shepherd. Here, the power of environment is strengthened by that of solitude—a spiritual asset of inestimable worth in any age, especially this one.

Of the physical kind, there is walking and rock-climbing. But it is that same power of environment which adds so greatly to the delights of both. Under another name this power is called 'natural scenery'. By a near association of word-sounds it is easy to confound 'scenery' with what can be 'seen'. But it is not the optical effect of scenery which matters so much as its effect on the imagination: and this is acted on through other senses besides that of vision. While the eye takes in the bold shapes of hills with their suggestiveness of mass and endurance, the long prospects and play of light on surfaces where colours match each setting in a perfect harmony that no human arrangement-organiser could produce, the lungs take in air that is clean, fragrant, and invigorating, and the ear subtleties of sound that cannot be translated into either words or music.

The first attempt to preserve the countryside in the good shape to which it had been brought by a long process of evolution, predominantly natural but partly artificial, was made in 1895 by the formation of the National Trust, a creation for which the initiative of three enthusiastic idealists was entirely responsible. In the same year Mrs. Talbot of Barmouth gave practical effect to the new body by making it a present of four and a half acres of land immediately behind her house. This property, called Dinas Oleu (the Castle of Light) lay along the high cliff top, overlooking Cader Idris, the Mawddach Estuary, and the whole sweep of Cardigan Bay—one of the grandest views in the British Isles. A small beginning but a great example! Today you may step directly from those few protected acres into the National Park, a protected area of nearly 850 square miles, established in 1951.

The National Trust and the National Park are, however, quite separate things not to be confounded with one another. The Trust is a large landowner. It owns the freehold of its properties and lets its farms on ordinary leases. The National Parks Authorities are not landowners but planning and controlling guardians. They derive their powers from the National Parks and Access to the Countryside Act of

1949, when the National Parks Commission was set up, and work in many ways to keep the Parks beautiful for our enjoyment. But the various Parks now established are not all administered in the same way. The Snowdonia Park comes under a Joint Advisory Committee on which the three counties of Merioneth, Caernarvon, and Denbigh are represented by eight, six, and two members respectively, together with eight members nominated by the Minister of Housing and Local Government. But each county has its own Park Planning Committee which is responsible for the administration of its own area.

The National Trust owns several properties, large and small, within the National Park. And there is yet another body concerned with preservation, though its first care is not either aesthetic or historic (except as regards the longer view of geological ages)—it is scientific. This third party is called the Nature Conservancy. To it is entrusted the safeguarding of wild life (plant and animal) and important geological features. It carries out its function mainly by observing and studying every aspect of plant and animal life within limited areas, a process requiring the compilation of records extending over a great many years. For that purpose it makes choice of places, already known for their outstanding interest, to which it gives special protection as *Nature Reserves*. Powers were given to establish and control these reserves under the same Act of 1949 which created the National Parks Commission. Nature Reserves are not confined to the National Parks, but three[1] have now been established in that of Snowdonia.

The first was at Lake Idwal (Plate IX) at the head of Nant Ffrancon Pass (page 66). It is held on a 99-year lease from the National Trust and thus under triple guardianship from all three public authorities. The second to be formed was at the other extreme end of the Park, in another deep hollow high up in a mountain side whose precipices are also lit by a lively, flashing little lake—Llyn Cau on the south face of Cader Idris (page 96). This has been granted in perpetuity to the Conservancy through the generosity of Mr. Ivor T. Idris. Each of these Reserves is a complete piece of scenery in itself which actually has living links with its principal sculptor, the glaciers of the Ice Age. Not only are the tooling marks plainly to be seen but also there has survived a persistent heritage of arctic-alpine flora.

The third is on the rugged escarpment overlooking Tremadoc, clothed from top to bottom with a shaggy oak wood, an almost untouched

[1] Five additional Reserves in the Park area have recently been announced. They are part of the sandy foreland at Morfa Harlech, Coed Camlyn south of Maentwrog, two woodlands of native hardwood trees in the Conway valley—Coed Dolgarrog and Gorswen—and the summits of Rhinog Fawr and Rhinog Fach.

survival of the primaeval forests of Wales—Coed Tremadoc (page 79). It has been leased to the Conservancy by Captain S. Livingstone-Learmonth. Probably other Reserves will follow before the next edition of the Guide is issued. While this authority sets out with an avowed aim different from the other two, its operations should have the same effect of preserving the natural scene which, in fact, can be thus guaranteed to be even more closely guarded. For that purpose wardens are appointed who are both keepers and knowledgeable purveyors of information.

The Forestry Commission has, for many years before the National Park was founded, been planting open hillsides or replanting existing woodlands in all parts of Wales. Some of its larger coniferous plantations are now within the National Park. The Snowdonia National Forest Park, formed in 1937, covers more than 22,000 acres and includes the two large forests of Gwydyr in the east and Beddgelert in the west, in connection with which the Forestry Commission issues its own Guide, noted on page 99.

Two things are characteristic of this age, and more particularly of this island. The conscious appreciation of natural beauty, and the rapidity with which natural beauty is being destroyed. . . . Like the Universe, like life, natural beauty also is a mystery. But whatever it may be, whether casual in its origin, as some hold who love it well, or whether as others hold such splendour can be nothing less than the purposeful message of God—whatever its interpretation may be, natural beauty is the ultimate spiritual appeal of the Universe, of nature, or of the God of nature, to their nursling man.

G. M. TREVELYAN

in the Rickman Godlee Lecture for 1931

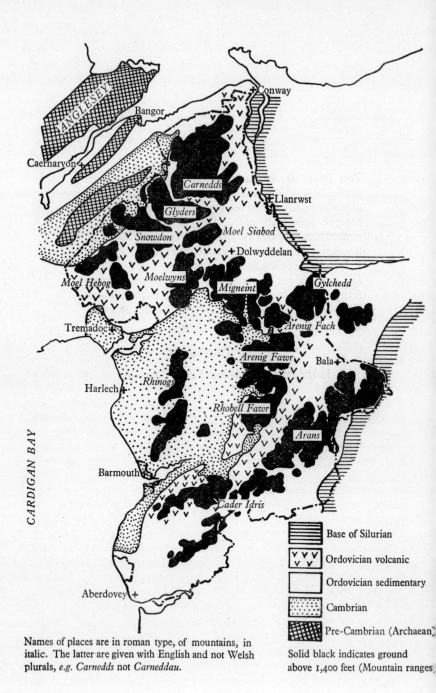

CARDIGAN BAY

ANGLESEY

Bangor

Caernarvon

Conway

Carnedds

Glyders

Llanrwst

Moel Siabod

Snowdon

Dolwyddelan

Moelwyns

Moel Hebog

Migneint

Gylchedd

Tremadoc

Arenig Fach

Arenig Fawr

Bala

Rhinogs

Harlech

Rhobell Fawr

Arans

Barmouth

Cader Idris

Aberdovey

Base of Silurian

V V V Ordovician volcanic

Ordovician sedimentary

Cambrian

Pre-Cambrian (Archaean)

Names of places are in roman type, of mountains, in italic. The latter are given with English and not Welsh plurals, *e.g. Carnedds* not *Carneddau*.

Solid black indicates ground above 1,400 feet (Mountain ranges

I

The Geology of the Park

by T. G. MILLER

GENERAL STRUCTURE

THE geological structure of North Wales is exceedingly complex, both in the diversity of its rock-types and also in the way in which these rocks are arranged. Fortunately the strong and rugged surface relief makes it possible to see much of the rock-fabric clearly exposed, and for certain parts of the National Park a great amount of highly detailed information has been accumulated over the last hundred years—since A. C. Ramsay's *Geological Survey Memoir* was published in 1866.

Although the complete form of the rock-masses is often difficult to make out, a generalized pattern can be recognized, and it is fairly easy to visualize a simple model on which to fix one's position in geological terms. The foundations of such a model lie outside the boundaries of the Park, in the surface rocks of Anglesey, and in two small mainland patches—between Bangor and Caernarvon, and between Bethesda and Pen-y-Groes. These are very ancient rocks, of the Pre-Cambrian (Archaean) 'basement complex', that farther to the south-east lie deeply buried, but come again to the surface along the English border beyond the Berwyns. The two mainland patches—formed, in effect, by two upward ripples in the Archaean floor—lie along the north-west edge of the Park, and against them to the south-east lies piled, also in crumpled folds, a great blanket of much newer rocks, that must at one time have stretched continuously across Anglesey and the Irish Sea, but whose worn-down edges now make the main mountain-land of Wales. Within this blanket (itself a series of separate layers) are two huge folds— or one complete fold, having both ridge and complementary trough— crossing the Park with long axes (or centre-lines) running south-west to north-east parallel to the 'grain' of Anglesey (seen in its river-lines and the Menai Strait) and the Archaean ridges of Bangor and Padarn. These two folds—the trough or *syncline* taking its name from Snowdon, which lies near its centre, and the arch, or dome, an *anticline* centred on the westward hills of Merioneth, and generally called the Harlech dome—dominate and control the position and attitude of the major rock-units of the whole region. The immediate effect is to preserve the youngest rocks of Snowdonia as a filling in the central part of the syncline, and to raise to the surface in the worn-down middle of the

I

Harlech anticline a much older rock-sequence. The real size of these structures is very great, for the wave-length of the folds is measured in miles and the amplitude in thousands of feet, while the thickness of distinguishable rock-units varies from several hundreds to several thousands of feet.

Taking the rock-blanket for the moment to be a series of simple layers, the general form of the fold-structure can be made out in a traverse across the Park from north to south. Along the north-western boundary the rocks slant ('dip' to the geologist, in degrees measured from the horizontal) south-east, away from the Archaean anticline of Llyn Padarn, going down into the centre of the Snowdon syncline, so that, passing to the south, successively higher (i.e. *younger*) layers in the sedimentary sequence appear in turn; beyond Snowdon, across the axis of the syncline, the dip-direction is reversed, and the layers come up again in reverse order as we pass outwards from the massif across Nant Gwynant towards Ffestiniog. With the layers (or 'beds') thus now dipping north-westerly we transfer from the southern flank of the Snowdon syncline to the northern flank of the Harlech dome, and the beds begin gradually to turn over, in the Merioneth uplands east of Trawsfynydd, across the top of the arch, until in the foothills of Rhobell Fawr, the Arans, and Cader Idris, they dip again to the south-east in the southern flank of the great anticline.

In our model it is necessary to have not only folds but also *fractures* on a very large scale running through the entire region. These fractures, planes of dislocation, or *faults*, sometimes tens of miles long and penetrating thousands of feet into the earth, are additional results of the same forces that folded our pile of rock blankets—the expression of the passing of a critical point or breaking strain in the whole fabric— causing adjacent slabs of the earth's crust to move relative to one another, either up, down, or sideways. Such movements nearly always produce shattering of the rocks along the plane of shift, and these planes, often cutting across the fold 'grain', may be expressed at the surface as lines of easy drainage or weathering, as ridge-lines or depressions, occasionally suspiciously straight, as in the case of the Tal-y-Llyn valley south of Cader Idris, which lies on one of the most important fracture lines of Wales—the Bala fault.

THE ROCKS THEMSELVES

It is comparatively easy to build up a model, but in reality the rocks show enormous variations, in structure, composition, texture, and distribution, and one or two of their more fundamental characters must be noticed here, since they control the actual 'look' of the rocks.

In a 'normal' assemblage of *sedimentary* rocks—i.e. those formed by the slow accumulation, usually on a sea- or lake-floor, of great sheets of mud, silt, sand, or gravel, now consolidated into mudstone, sandstone, or conglomerate—the most important physical character is the original layering, or bedding, nearly always assumed to have been originally horizontal, so that the dip we now see is a direct indication of tilting or folding. Unfortunately both these processes—tilting and folding—and the original consolidation of the rock, themselves induce other characters which may tend to obscure or even obliterate the original bedding. The two most important of these secondary structures are *jointing* and *cleavage*, and the effect of these, together with the bedding, usually determines the particular shape and expression of a rock at the surface.

Early in the life-history of a sedimentary rock much rearrangement of its constituent material takes place by means of the simple weight of younger layers accumulating above it—for example, water is driven out of the spaces between sand-grains—and later there develop strong forces that shift the bedding from its original horizontality. Within the rock the effect of these forces is to produce a system of potential cracks, or directions of preferred splitting, as regularly arranged (i.e. roughly parallel) sets of internal plane or slightly curved surfaces. These 'joint planes' usually make high angles with the bedding, and if there are two sets at right-angles to each other, and to the bedding, the rock breaks into regular blocks or slabs, and tends to have an 'architectural' appearance. Joints thus frequently control the shape of exposed rock surfaces—slab, gully, or pinnacle, as it may happen.

Cleavage involves a much more severe internal distortion of the rock, and is produced by intense and prolonged external pressure and probably also some heat. These factors produce upon the original assemblage of sand-grains, silt-particles, clay-mineral flakes and needles, or the crystal pieces of a volcanic ash, a gross internal physical deformation —a re-orientation—tending to diminish the external stress by turning the particles into planes at right-angles to the direction in which the stress is acting. These new planes, *entirely independent of the original bedding*, become the planes of cleavage, whose closeness of packing depends only on the grain-size of the particles making the rock. When cleavage is imposed on a rock of suitably fine and homogeneous texture —smooth uniform mudstones for example—true *slates* are produced, which will split into familiar thin grey and purple slabs, as in the great Welsh slate belts of Bethesda, Llanberis, Nantlle, and Ffestiniog. These rocks will only rarely split along the bedding, and usually the combination of cleavage and jointing makes the whole rock particularly 'rotten' and liable to break into small, flat, parallel-sided pieces, and to form narrow sloping ridges ('house-roof' shapes) and pinnacles where it is exposed to weathering on high ground.

So far we have mentioned only the sedimentary rocks. In North Wales the succession has been complicated by the introduction of a great series of *igneous* rocks, and the products of igneous—i.e. volcanic—activity. Most of these are either volcanic lavas, ejected as 'flows' from vents that seem often to have been under the sea; or great sheets of volcanic *ash*, also blown out of vents, sometimes bedded, mixed with mud, and containing fossils; or they may be masses of rock, sometimes sheet-like, sometimes quite irregular, that were *injected* (or *intruded*) as fluids or semi-fluids into the already formed and consolidated stack of rock-layers. These last, the intrusive igneous rocks, with the volcanic lavas and certain of the ashes, are *crystalline*—made of a more or less tightly interlocking mosaic of individual mineral crystals grown in and from a molten mass: whereas the sedimentary rocks are made of separate mineral grains derived from some pre-existing source, accumulated individually, and usually stratified or bedded.

All this great multi-layered sandwich of variegated rocks, at least five miles thick in the Park area, has been crumpled and compressed into the tortuous fold- and fracture-system we see today, the original or primary structures often modified or obliterated by the imposition of cleavage and jointing, and the fundamentally simple pattern of successive layers distorted by the effects of volcanic explosions and the subsequent injection of streams of molten rock into the whole pile.

GEOLOGICAL HISTORY

We have now outlined the main characters of the rocks that go to setting the shape of the Park's surface features: it remains to consider the present form of the mountain-groups and the dividing valleys and passes—the accumulated results of hundreds of millions of years of earth-history. During this tremendous span of time North Wales has been alternately buried under layers of sedimentary rock and elevated into the zone in which erosion is stronger than deposition. Some time within the last hundred million years it is probable that the drainage pattern was established, not as we see it now in detail, but in its essential basic shape. The latest, and for us the most significant major phase in the historical process, was the establishment, about one million years ago, of a great ice-sheet over Scandinavia, the North Sea, and Scotland, whose marginal lobes penetrated down the depression of the Irish Sea and across the Cheshire plain. At the same time in North Wales small valley glaciers developed, and coalesced into a local sheet with a centre in Merioneth east of the Arenigs. This 'native'

Welsh ice-cap was able to push back and deflect the invading stream from the north along the seaward margin of Snowdonia. The great main continental ice was probably six or eight thousand feet thick at its centre over the northern Baltic Sea; the Welsh one cannot have reached much more than a third of this, but the effects of its presence are seen all over the Park, both in valley bottoms and high on the mountain shoulders.

The main effects are two, and complementary: on the one hand the ice streams scoured off the weathered crust of rock-débris that in normal times accumulates on a land surface, exposing the fresh bedrock in deepened valleys and sharply cut-off ridge-shoulders; and on the other hand by redistributing all the torn-up and ground-down material round the ice-margin, and by dumping it from the finally melting ice, caused the blanketing and concealing of the bedrock under a new mantle of unconsolidated sand, silt, mud, gravel, and peat—what the field geologist calls *drift*.

The gathering-grounds of the Welsh glaciers may be seen today, emptied of their ice, as the upland amphitheatres of the main mountain massifs—the line of cwms along Nant Ffrancon and the north slopes of the Glyders, for example. The flow-lines of the glaciers can be seen in many grooved, scratched and polished rock-pavements in valley bottoms and along lower hill-slopes; many of the valleys have been over-deepened and now hold lakes like Llyn Peris, Llyn Padarn, or Llyn Ogwen, or have suffered 'unnatural' straightening by the sawing off of projecting hill-spurs. Within the mountain groups the débris from the final melting, which took place within the last twenty thousand years, lies piled in *moraines*—ridges, mounds and sheets of jumbled boulders, gravel, and sand along and across valleys and over the high table-lands, often damming up drainage lines to form lakes—of which the two Marchlyns between Llanberis and Nant Ffrancon are an example.

Round the edges of the mountains the unconsolidated glacial deposits were originally dumped in much greater quantity, and remain now spread over the lowlands and plastered over the foothills in Arvon, through the Caernarvon-Pwllheli-Criccieth gap, and among the isolated hills of Llcyn. The sequence of boulder-filled silts and clays alternating with laminated sands and gravels is exposed in the cliffs of Cardigan Bay. Identification of boulders and pebbles in these beds makes possible the tracing of the flow-lines of the Irish and Scottish ice-stream—pieces of the famous Ailsa Craig microgranite of the Firth of Clyde, granites from Cumberland and Westmorland, blocks of limestone and flint and masses of gravel with sea-shells that can only have come from the floor of the Irish Sea, all these have clearly been torn from their native places and carried far to the south. But the Irish

Sea ice never penetrated the 'sanctuary' of North Wales, and within the sanctuary only local rocks are found scattered down the valleys, the stranger-boulders being restricted to the east and west borders.

In time following, probably after a long interval, and in space overlying or leaning upon, the old Archaean foundation of the Padarn strip, come the various members of the great succession of fossil-bearing strata (there are no Archaean fossils), which the geologist for convenience divides into groups labelled with 'dynastic' names in the style of the familiar historical equivalents—Saxon, Norman, Plantaganet—which are used instead of numerical dates to identify events and situations. The rock-dynasties of Caernarvonshire and Merioneth, their names appropriately of Welsh origin, are the *Cambrian, Ordovician,* and *Silurian.*

(i) *Cambrian*

The Cambrian rocks occupy two separate areas. The northern is a five-mile-wide strip running, in the Anglesey 'grain', from Clynnog Fawr on the coast across the three Snowdon passes, and fading out in the slopes of Moel Wnion, north-east of Bethesda. The southern area occupies the quadrilateral Harlech—Blaenau Ffestiniog—Dolgelley —Barmouth and is the core of the great Harlech anticline.

The Cambrian of Arvon forms the edge of the Park, skirting the great slate-mining centres of Penrhyn-Bethesda, Llanberis and Nantlle, where smooth even-grained purple and green Cambrian mudstones have been nipped and cleaved between the old Archaean ridge rocks and the great mass of the Snowdonian Ordovician to the south. Between Nant Ffrancon and Nant Peris Cambrian strata above the slates stand out as prominent ridges—Elidir Fawr and Fach, and Carnedd-y-Filiast— built of hard pebbly well-bedded sandstones which continue south-west to the summits of Moel Tryfan, Pen-y-Cilgwyn, and the heights overlooking Llyn Cwellyn from the west. Occasional bedding surfaces of these rocks show perfect ripple-marks—fossilized Cambrian sea-floors; others are covered with sinuous ropey marks and lines of indentations—the casts and burrows of worms, and the tracks of some unknown crawling beasts of the Cambrian sea. But in general there are few fossils to be found in the Cambrian strata.

The Merioneth Cambrian quadrilateral centres physically on the Rhinog mountains—the irregular long north-south ridge running from Moel Penoleu through the Rhinogs and Y Llethr to Llawr Llech, with Moelfre and Y Garn as wings to west and east. All this country west of the Trawsfynydd road is based on much the same kinds of thickly bedded hard and massive gritstones as we see in Arvon, producing a rather desolate region of stepped terraces bounded by steep lines of crag running up to the main peaks. Round the central grit mass the higher Cambrian beds, shalier and softer, often weathering in rusty colours, underlie much of the moorland that stretches east towards the Arenigs. Here the bare crags are nearly all igneous rocks that have been injected as sheets and tongues into the main sedimentary sequence. Associated with some of them are the gold- and copper-bearing lodes said to have been worked by the Romans at various places in the streams draining to the Mawddach. Gold was still being extracted at the end of the last century, and patient panning will still turn up a flake or two at certain spots.

(ii) *Ordovician*

Above the Cambrian strata, both in the Snowdon passes and on the landward sides of the Harlech dome, comes a great thickness of Ordovician rocks, making a roughly S-shaped outcrop through Snowdonia and southwards by the Moelwyns and the Migneint to the arc of the Arenigs, the Arans, and Cader Idris. The great feature of this region lies in the evidence it provides of a huge outpouring of volcanic material, both as fluid lava-streams and as great blankets of ash, in Ordovician times, about four hundred million years ago. The solid remnants of these ancient Welsh volcanoes, now stripped to their roots, twisted and distorted out of all likeness to a modern volcanic island-chain, has been called the Ordovician 'Ring of Fire'. Naturally, however much some of the present peaks may look like symmetrical volcanic cones, none of them has ever in this sense been a volcano, and the original structures have long since been flattened and destroyed by erosion.

The massifs of the Glyders, Snowdon, and the northern fringe of the Hebog Range are carved out of the typical Ordovician succession, magnificently displayed along the passes of Nant Ffrancon, Llanberis, Nant Gwynant and Drws-y-Coed. There are innumerable complications produced by intense local folding and fracturing, superimposed on the main structure, but the general arrangement continues the Anglesey 'grain', of strips lying stretched from south-west to north-east across the valley lines. The base of the sequence—seen, for example, in the screes above Llyn Dwythwch, south of Llanberis—is usually a gritty or pebbly rock containing an abnormal amount of the mineral *tourmaline*, and occasional phosphatized lumps of the curious polyzoan fossil *Bolopora undosa*, but most of the purely sedimentary rocks of the Ordovician are fine-grained, rather soft, dark-grey or almost black shales, usually intensely cleaved, and with a peculiar irregular 'rubbly' texture. The peaks of Yr Aran and Y Graigwen are built of these slates, which in some places are so full of the mineral *pyrite* that they carry a coating of rust from its decomposition. The bedding is generally concealed by the cleavage, and consequently any animal remains, which would normally lie along the bedding planes, having settled down on to a flat sea-floor and there been buried by mud or silt, are difficult to see. However, chance is occasionally kind to fossils, and *graptolites*, looking like bits of small hacksaw blade, can be found, for example near the Snowdon Ranger; and *brachiopods*, somewhat like distorted cockle-shells, and *corals*, in the dark brownish-green ashy rock on Snowdon summit.

Throughout this region the main mountain masses are built round the far harder rocks of igneous origin. These include rather finely crystalline lavas often showing peculiar structures produced by their having been ejected on to the sea-floor, or into semi-liquid muds just below it—the 'pillow-structure' so splendidly displayed near the top of the Devil's Kitchen; or through having been sufficiently thick and massive to develop, on cooling, regular joints in three sets inclined at 60° to form hexagonal columns, as on the Lliwedd ridge; or by reason of their original viscosity showing 'flow-banding' or nodule-structure as at Pitt's Head. In other cases the rocks are stratified, and are interpreted not as primary igneous rocks, but as ashy material ejected from the volcanic vents and accumulated in more or less regular beds either on the exposed slopes of the volcanoes themselves, or more usually in the sea-waters surrounding or even covering the vents—all now consolidated into hard massive sheets of various compositions and textures, well displayed, for example, on Lliwedd and Llechog. Occasionally, as in the crags of Cwm Idwal, they contain a good deal of limey or chalky matter, and there is a strong contrast between the rich green ferns and mosses growing on them and the patches of heather and bilberry of the more acid rocks below.

Much of the lower upland at or a little below 2,000 feet east and south of the Snowdon group is based on the relatively soft main sedimentary Ordovician sequence, most of the isolated hills being centred on hard, often irregular, igneous intrusions. Moel Siabod to the north, Cynicht and the Moelwyns to the south, are of this kind; and the mountains between Tremadoc and Beddgelert are a complex of similar igneous injections together with others associated with almost horizontal fracture-planes that convert the whole mass into a jumble of igneous and sedimentary layers, and belts of shattered mixtures. An additional effect, seen particularly in the country round Ffestiniog, is the appearance in the country-rock of a network of hard white quartz veins, which stand out on weathered surfaces, seeming to bind the rock in a tight irregular mesh.

Towards the Arenigs the high ground reverts very largely to the 'Snowdon' structure—fairly regular alternation of bedded volcanic ashes and true lava flows—and this great series, in part at least older than that of Snowdon, carries on the 'Ring of Fire' in a southern arc that reaches the sea at Towyn, north of Aberdovey.

The eastern flank and summit of Arenig Fawr, like Snowdon, is formed of a thick bed of ash, with jointing on a rather large scale, producing fantastic shapes on weathering; while the north side, the crags of Maen-grygog and Daear Fawr, are of crystalline, occasionally columnar jointed primary igneous rock. On Arenig Fach the stratification is particularly well shown as long terraces on the western and northern crags, where short lens-shaped patches of slate, more easily weathered than the lavas, are interspersed among the ashes. The precipitous east side of Moel Llyfnant, farther south, shows similar terracing in well-bedded fine sandstones full of fossil worm-tracks and castings.

The most southerly sector of the volcanic arc, before it is cut off by the sea, is the east-west range of Cader Idris, whose great bare scarp face looks north across the Mawddach estuary to the Cambrian rocks in the core of the Harlech anticline. The rock succession is remarkably regular from north to south through the main part of the lower and middle Ordovician, dipping steadily south or south-west at about 40°. Only near the summit where softer mudstones appear are any sharp folds developed. Going up by the Fox's Path the first major group of lavas makes the prominent feature between Llyn-y-Gader and Llyn-y-Gafr, and the same rocks occupy the whole of the upland valley between Mynydd-y-Gader and Mynydd Moel. Each separate lava flow tends to have columnar jointing in its middle part, and to become 'pillowy' on its upper surface, often with considerable masses of slate between the pillows. Close above this lava group, along the base of the main scarp, there is a seam of iron ore which has been worked at its continuation near Cross Foxes, towards Dolgelley. The upper group of volcanic rocks begins with a massive ash bed which caps the cliffs of Pen-y-Gader, above the lake, and the lavas above form the actual summit of Cader Idris and the rough dip-slope running down to Llyn Cau.

. South of the main range the ground on both sides of the Tal-y-Llyn valley is occupied by a rather featureless series of highly cleaved mudstones and siltstones. These, with the addition of occasional gritty and limey bands form all the country round the south and east margins of the Park. Except for the ridge of the Tarens between the Tal-y-Llyn and Dovey valleys, and around Maesglasau west of Dinas Mawddwy, where there are high-level rocky cwms, these rocks express themselves as comparatively subdued country with rounded hill-forms and thickly wooded valley-slopes. Into this softer and more domesticated 'rim' detached outposts of the Arenig volcanic arc project—Gylchedd and Mynydd Nodol 'standing apart like outraged keystones beyond the centre of the arch'.

(iii) *Silurian*

Little need be said about the small areas of Silurian rocks that fall within the boundaries of the Park. They lie between Betws-y-Coed and Pentre Foelas on the north-east side, south-east of Bala (above Aber Hirnant), and south of Llanymawddwy on the slopes of Tir Rhiwiog. All these small patches continue the rather monotonous subdued pattern of the upper Ordovician mudstone region that encircles the mountain nuclei, much of it moorland with stretches of peaty ground, part densely afforested, and in relatively few places showing outcrops of solid rock. Whenever they can be seen the rocks are mainly shales or fine-grained sandstones, usually strongly cleaved, and often showing a distinctive stripey lamination in pale grey and green tints. Above Aber Hirnant, on the extreme south-west tip of the Berwyn ridge, these rocks form the synclinal trough (complementary to the Harlech anticline) that bounds the next anticlinal arch to the east, the Berwyn dome, which brings the familiar volcanic Ordovician rocks to the surface again.

THE INTRUSIVE ROCKS

Compared with the structurally similar areas of Ireland and Scotland and the English Lake District, North Wales is deficient in large bodies of intrusive igneous rock—compact masses like those of Wicklow, Shap, or Criffel. Probably the most prominent of the much smaller Welsh examples is the great sheet, or 'sill', of granitic composition, that forms the line of cliffs from Cyfrwy to Mynydd Moel in the scarp front of Cader Idris. This sill shows perfectly the development of joint-bounded columns crossing the sheet from top to bottom. It is a geologic oddity that whereas this sill forms such a prominent feature on Cader Idris, another, very similar, one lower down in the succession forms the broad upland *hollow* between the scarp and the Mawddach estuary.

North of the Vale of Ffestiniog and throughout Snowdonia, thin sheets of injected igneous rock occur among both the soft sedimentary rocks and interleaved with the much harder lavas and ashes. It becomes difficult to distinguish the three kinds of rock—lava, ash, and sill-rock—particularly when their tops or bottoms are concealed. On theoretical grounds the distinctions are straightforward enough—a sill, being injected as a hot fluid, heats and slightly bakes the sandwiching rocks both above and below; a lava, being an ejected fluid, can only bake the rock below it, and often has slaggy surfaces; an ash bed would not normally have any baking effect at all, and may be stratified. But where the three kinds recur and alternate, and have suffered folding and cleavage and a variety of other secondary alterations, even the most experienced geologist may have to think twice.

However, there are certain other intrusions that are comparatively easy to recognize—the granitic rocks (microgranites and 'felsites') of Crib-goch and Crib-y-Ddisgl on Snowdon; the Bwlch-y-Cywion granite on the precipitous ridge of Y Llwmllwyd; the riebeckite-microgranite of Mynydd Mawr; the Tan-y-Grisiau granite near Ffestiniog; and many other smaller bodies of rock that were originally driven up as fluids through the main pile of sedimentary and volcanic layers. They are all crystalline, fairly even-textured throughout, never stratified, and usually show a joint-pattern different from that of the enclosing rocks. They are mentioned after the sedimentary 'dynasties' because they are later in time, having been emplaced when the 'host' rocks were already formed and consolidated.

THE GEOLOGICAL TIME-SCALE

The figures shown below as ages in millions of years are approximations: the error involved increases with increasing age but the beginning of the Cambrian period was probably between 400 and 600 million years ago.

Cenozoic periods:	Pleistocene or Glacial	Unconsolidated gravels, sands and clays, often with large boulders ('erratics'), and containing remains of early Man.

1 million years————————————————————————

	Pliocene Miocene Oligocene Eocene Palaeocene	Soft sands and clays, only occasionally cemented as hard rock, with rare bands of limestone confined to South and South-east England.

70 million years————————————————————————

Mesozoic periods:	Cretaceous Jurassic	Yellow and greenish - grey sandstones, grey clays, grey and creamy-yellow limestones, and pure white limestone (chalk). Probably forming part of the Irish Sea floor.
	Triassic	Bright red sandstones and pebble-beds.

190 million years————————————————————————

Palaeozoic periods:

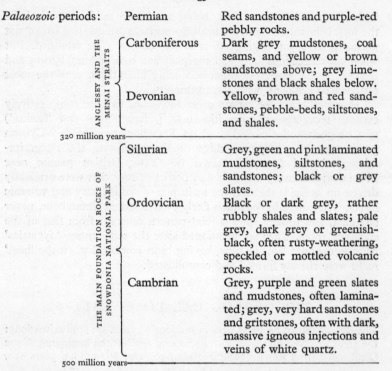

	Permian	Red sandstones and purple-red pebbly rocks.
ANGLESEY AND THE MENAI STRAITS	Carboniferous	Dark grey mudstones, coal seams, and yellow or brown sandstones above; grey limestones and black shales below.
	Devonian	Yellow, brown and red sandstones, pebble-beds, siltstones, and shales.

320 million years

THE MAIN FOUNDATION ROCKS OF SNOWDONIA NATIONAL PARK	Silurian	Grey, green and pink laminated mudstones, siltstones, and sandstones; black or grey slates.
	Ordovician	Black or dark grey, rather rubbly shales and slates; pale grey, dark grey or greenish-black, often rusty-weathering, speckled or mottled volcanic rocks.
	Cambrian	Grey, purple and green slates and mudstones, often laminated; grey, very hard sandstones and gritstones, often with dark, massive igneous injections and veins of white quartz.

500 million years

Pre-Cambrian (Archaean) rocks, not subdivided into periods:

Very much contorted mainly grey and green rocks of various sedimentary types including red jasper, with granitic and basaltic injections and black or green mottled volcanic rocks. The 'basement complex' of Anglesey and Lleyn, the ridge on which Bangor is built, and the adjoining one south which lies at the foot of the mountains.

2

Plant Life

by P. W. RICHARDS

THERE are about 2,000 different kinds of flowering plants in the whole of the British Isles and of these perhaps 900 grow in the Snowdonia National Park, as well as many ferns, mosses and other non-flowering plants. To write a comprehensive guide to the flora of Snowdonia would thus be to write a guide to nearly half the British flora. In a few pages nothing like this is possible; all that can be done is to sketch in barest outline a few of the most important features of the plant life.

At least one plant is found nowhere else in Britain but in Snowdonia. This is the Mountain Spiderwort (*Lloydia serotina*) (Plate II(*a*)), a delicate lily-like flower which, though very rare, grows on rock ledges in a few of the cwms of Snowdon and the Glyder range. But an abundance of rare or unusual plants is not characteristic of Snowdonia. A very large proportion of the area is rough enclosed or unenclosed hill pasture on which plant life is neither rich nor varied; only a few small moorland flowers break the general monotony and these are plants of poor acid soils which can be found in any part of the country where there are commons or hill grazings offering these conditions. Besides such moorland species most of the other plants which the ordinary country walker thinks of as common, such as Bluebells, Primroses and Foxgloves, are here too, but sometimes, in rather odd situations. The Bluebell, for instance, which in the home counties is almost exclusively a carpeter of woodlands, grows here in the open; the rough brackeny pastures of Nant Ffrancon and many other valleys are blue with it in early May. The Pink Campion, often a hedgerow plant, grows unexpectedly on the 'hanging gardens' of Cwm Idwal at 2,000 feet and is indeed unusually fine there in size and colouring. Some plants, however, which in most of England and Wales are common, are scarce in Snowdonia or missing altogether, for example the White Dead Nettle.

A typical scene in the National Park would include grassy hills, open above the 'mountain wall', enclosed pasture below it, precipitous rocky cliffs overhanging the cwms, and, much lower, patches of oakwood surviving from the far more extensive woods which a few centuries ago clothed nearly all the hillsides up to at least 1,000 feet. The plants to be mentioned first should be those which can be seen any day, anywhere in a Snowdonian landscape such as this. Afterwards there must be a few words about the true mountain plants, the 'alpines' which for many plant-lovers are one of the chief attractions of the National Park.

The hill grasslands whether enclosed or not are always sheep-grazed and even if the sheep, reckoned as so many to the acre, are very few, they always have a dominating influence on the plant life; it is because of the sheep that plants other than grasses, rushes and sedges tend to be few, and plants which cannot stand continual nibbling become restricted to places which the sheep cannot reach. Thus there are many hundreds of square miles of Welsh hill land which would be dreary enough, but for the little blue Milkwort, the four-petalled yellow Tormentil and the tiny whitish flowers of the Heath Bedstraw, which provide some contrast to the prevailing browns and dull greens of the moorland grasses.

Among the plants which are soon suppressed by grazing is the heather (*Calluna vulgaris*); consequently, though in Scotland dark heather-covered hills are a typical feature of the scenery, in Wales there is little heather except on slopes too steep and rocky to be grazed. The only parts of the National Park where heather grows luxuriantly and covers large areas are places like the upper slopes of Cwm Bychan near Harlech, or the few hills which are now, or were formerly, kept as grouse moors. If heather seldom makes a show, the same is not true of gorse, especially the dwarf, summer-flowering species (*Ulex gallii*) which covers many Welsh hillsides and which the hill farmer regards as one of the more pestilential weeds with which he has to contend.

Wet or boggy places offer more variety of plants than the drier, closely grazed slopes, and in the ill-drained valleys of mountain streams some of the most delightful flowers of the National Park can be found, such as the pale Pink Spotted Orchid (*Orchis ericetorum*), the yellow Bog St. Johnswort (*Hypericum elodes*) with its scarlet tipped buds, the fairy-like Ivy-leaved Bellflower (*Wahlenbergia hederacea*), the Bog Asphodel and the two insect-eating plants, the Butterwort with its deep purple flowers like violets and rosette of pale yellowish green leaves, and the Sundew, which has tiny roundish leaves covered with bright red sticky hairs. In more extensive boggy areas on low ground, such as the marshy fields by such rivers as the Ogwen and the Glaslyn, an attractive plant is the Bog Myrtle (*Myrica gale*) which looks like a knee-high willow but may be known by its delightfully aromatic leaves and catkins. The latter, which expand in April, are charming to look at but seldom noticed.

Several beautiful plants are particularly fond of the rocky beds of small streams which make their way in gulleys down steep hillsides;

two which may be mentioned are the Golden Saxifrage (*Chrysosplenium oppositifolium*), which flowers in spring and grows in brilliant green masses, and the much less common Starry Saxifrage (*Saxifraga stellaris*) which has tiny pinkish-white flowers like those of the London Pride.

Hill pastures of rough grasses with the other plants just mentioned intermingled, extend to the tops of the highest mountains; even on the summit of Cader Idris and on Snowdon and the Carneddau above 3,000 feet, the flora is much the same except that there are more stones, more moss and more bare ground than lower down. There is however, a true 'alpine' flora in Snowdonia; it is not found on the highest ridges and summits, but on the rock ledges of the precipitous cwms, especially those which face north and are consequently comparatively little exposed to the drying effects of direct sunshine. It is here that we find two of the saxifrages, the Purple Saxifrage (*Saxifraga oppositifolia*) (Plate II(*b*)), a dwarf moss-like plant with disproportionately large flowers of a rich purplish red, and the later-flowering pure white Mossy Saxifrage (*Saxifraga hypnoides*). The flowers of the former open in many years as early as the end of February and are much the earliest of the mountain flowers. Among many other plants which like these rock ledges are the Moss Campion (*Silene acaulis*) with its cheerful pink flowers embedded in a huge moss-like cushion and the Rose-root (*Sedum rosea*) a fleshy plant nine inches or more high whose thick brown rootstock when broken smells of roses. One of the handsomest of these 'alpines' is the Globe Flower (*Trollius europaeus*), which is like a large buttercup in which the flowers never open, the petals remaining curved into a ball; here and there it grows in the valleys as well as on mountain ledges. All these plants are found chiefly on rocks which contain some lime, such as the basic volcanic ash of Cader and Snowdon. On the screes below the mountain cliffs the Parsley Fern (*Cryptogramme crispa*) with densely tufted leaves, bright green in summer and russet brown in winter is highly characteristic.

These 'alpine' plants belong to a group with an interesting history. Botanists speak of them as 'Arctic-alpine' because outside the British Isles their chief homes are the Alps and the Arctic regions. With us they grow only on the higher mountains of Wales, northern England, Scotland and Ireland; when and how they got there has long been an interesting problem to plant geographers. It is fairly certain (from the study of fossil seeds, pollen, leaves, etc., in peat, lake muds, etc.) that these arctic-alpine plants were once much more widespread and grew in such far from mountainous districts as East Anglia and the Midlands. That however was some thousands of years ago in the early post-glacial period which followed the retreat of the great glaciers of the Ice Age. In later prehistoric times the country became warmer and much of it

became covered with forest, but the cwms of Snowdonia remained
treeless and continued to provide the cool, moist unshaded conditions
such plants need. Thus they are still here today while over most of the
country they have long disappeared.

As witnesses of the past as well as for their special beauty these
plants have a special claim to protection. They do not multiply quickly
or readily recover from disturbance, and it is much to be hoped that
climbers and other visitors to the National Park will learn to recognize
them but leave them undisturbed.

Some plants, including the woodland species referred to earlier,
habitually grow on the same ledges as the arctic-alpines. One rarity
which may be mentioned here is the yellow-flowered Welsh Poppy
(*Meconopsis cambrica*); though not a native of either the Arctic or the
Alps it grows on the rock ledges inhabited by the arctic-alpines on several
mountains of Snowdonia.

The natural woodlands of Snowdonia are mainly Oak (usually
Sessile Oak, *Quercus petraea*), though other trees such as Ash, Birch,
Wych Elm (*Ulmus glabra*) and Mountain Ash (*Sorbus aucuparia*) are
common, not to mention many non-native species such as the Sycamore.
Isolated trees, especially Mountain Ash, Ash and Oak often grow on
crags out of reach of sheep and probably testify to the former existence
of woodlands at much higher altitudes than at the present day. The
natural woodlands have decreased to mere relics and are still
diminishing. To an increasing extent they are being cleared to make
room for plantations of Larch, Sitka Spruce and other conifers. Though
from an economic point of view this may be a gain, the incomparable
beauty of the oakwoods still remaining in the valleys would be an
irretrievable loss were all of them to be replaced by non-indigenous
conifers.

Most of the Snowdonian woods are rather open and the ground
under the trees is often overgrown with grass and moorland plants rather
than typical woodland undergrowth. The reason for this is mainly
sheep or cattle grazing; the woods play an important part in the hill
farmer's economy by providing winter shelter. Apart from the usual
moorland plants, a flower very characteristic of the oakwoods is the
Cow Wheat (*Melampyrum pratense*) which carpets the ground with
gold in late summer.

Damper woods, especially on steep slopes near streams (which are
often little grazed) have an altogether richer and more varied flora.
A variety of ferns is often found here—Male Fern, Lady Fern, Mountain
Buckler and many others; these are a particularly delightful feature of
the Snowdonian valleys, especially in spring when the young fronds
are unfolding.

The Snowdonia National Park does not consist of hills and valleys only. The sand dunes of Mochras and Morfa Harlech have a delightful flora quite different from that found inland and even the muddy and pebbly stretches of coast which are found here and there between Traeth Mawr and the Dovey Estuary are the home of many interesting and attractive plants. The sand dune plants are at their best in the late spring and early summer when the yellow, blue and particoloured Dune Pansies (*Viola curtisii*) are flowering everywhere; at that season, too, many tiny gem-like flowers are found, minute Forget-me-nots, Cranesbills and many more. Later in the year the swampy hollows or 'slacks' between dunes become the chief attraction because of the abundance of Marsh Orchids, Marsh Helleborine and other beautiful plants, as well as those which are more rare but less striking to the eye. Because of the special interest of the plant life (as well as the animals associated with it) it is hoped that at least two of these sand dune areas will become nature reserves in the care of the Nature Conservancy. To the lover of plants the coast is by no means the least of the attractions of the Snowdonia National Park.

Research. The plant life of Snowdonia has been the subject of scientific study ever since its special interest became known through the adventurous journeys of Thomas Johnson, John Ray, Edward Lhwyd and others in the seventeenth and eighteenth centuries. Today such work is carried out mainly by the staffs of the Botany Departments of the University Colleges at Bangor and Aberystwyth and the Welsh Regional Office of the Nature Conservancy in Bangor, but knowledge of Snowdonian plants still owes much to visitors from outside Wales. Owing to their accessibility and botanical interest Snowdonia in the narrow sense and Cader Idris are both favourite places for visiting parties of university students and are thus important training grounds for the plant scientists of the future. There is some danger that plants so much loved and studied will suffer from inconsiderate destruction; long may they survive to serve for the study and enjoyment of future generations!

3

The Fauna of the Park

by F. W. R. BRAMBELL

THE mountains of Snowdonia are one of the greatest remaining sanctuaries for those wilder members of the British fauna which have retreated in front of industrialization and mechanized agriculture. Here are to be found in fair numbers some of those animals which were once spread throughout Britain, but which are now only to be seen in the fastnesses of the north and west and which have survived there from the earliest times. Amongst them are some of the more interesting of our wild animals, but with the development of access to the more remote regions of the Park, their survival must depend increasingly on positive measures of protection and encouragement. They constitute for many people a principal attraction, adding much to the interest and enjoyment of the National Park but owing their continued existence to the good will of the public, both residents and visitors alike, and to an enlightened policy of conservation. These animals delight in the sheer extent of the uninhabited or sparsely inhabited regions of mountain, moorland and forest rather than in otherwise unique habitats. Some animals, however, are comparatively undisturbed by man and others are attracted by his presence; for some of these the Park is also a greatly favoured haunt, but for another reason. The area is as remarkable for the diversity of habitats which it provides as for the extent of some of these. Mountains and valleys, moorlands and forests, cliffs, quarries and screes, highland and lowland lakes, torrents, streams and sluggish rivers, marshes, saltings and estuaries, and to the north and west, the sea, with its islands and varied coast, together comprise a number of environments which it would be hard to equal in any area of similar extent. Yet each environment is peopled by its own characteristic inhabitants as well as by those which are less exacting and more widespread.

MAMMALS

Foxes abound throughout the Park and are especially numerous in the more mountainous and wooded areas—often they are so plentiful as to be a serious pest to farmers, especially in the lambing season, although large numbers are killed annually, to keep them in check.

18

PLATE II (*a*). The Mountain Spider-Wort (Lloydia serotina)

PLATE II (*b*). The purple Saxifrage (Saxifraga oppositifolia)

PLATE III (*a*). Wild Ponies on the Carnedd Range

PLATE III (*b*). Grey Seal, Cardigan Bay

Otters also are numerous in the larger rivers, and badgers are common in many wooded districts. They would be still more numerous if they were left unmolested, as they deserve. Although as a rule harmless and, indeed, useful animals, badgers are liable to be blamed for the sins of an occasional rogue.

Snowdonia is one of the remaining strongholds of that most beautiful and elusive of our native carnivores, the pine marten. Still an uncommon animal, it is nevertheless fairly widespread throughout the Park, though so shy and skilful in concealment as to be rarely seen. Once nearing extinction, it appears to be gradually increasing in numbers with the decline of game preservation. It is to be hoped that, with more enlightened public opinion and a greater appreciation of the attraction which the fauna and flora of the Park could provide, it will be given every encouragement and may perhaps in time become as numerous as it was before the advent of firearms and gin traps. Another carnivore, rather more numerous in Caernarvonshire and Merioneth-shire, and perhaps even increasing, is the polecat. Admittedly harmful to game and poultry, the polecat does much good in destroying large numbers of rabbits, rats and mice. Weighing the good against the bad, and taking account of its rarity elsewhere, it could well be encouraged to increase here, in its principal remaining stronghold in Wales. Stoats and weasels are numerous throughout the area. Sometimes in winter the stoat may be seen in its snow-white coat with only the tip of the tail black; the traditional 'ermine'. Despite occasional reports of wild cats, always traceable to domestic cats which have gone wild, the true wild cat has long been extinct in Wales, as has also the wolf.

Deer are virtually absent from Snowdonia, only very occasional strays appearing at long intervals and failing to establish themselves. Their place is taken by goats, several herds of which roam wild over the mountains. Although such herds have been present for a long time and maintain themselves by breeding, they are of feral[1] origin and have, doubtless, been augmented at frequent intervals by strays from domestication. Probably they owe their origin to the long established custom in this, as in several other mountainous districts of Britain, of grazing goats with cattle on the mountains, so that they should eat the luscious bits on the more inaccessible ledges, thereby preventing the less agile cattle from being tempted to hazard themselves in dangerous places. These feral goats become very shaggy and well horned, and each herd is led, as a rule, by a magnificent old male. It is a splendid sight to see such a herd outlined far above against the sky-line or moving away from an intruder, sure footed, across a precipitous

[1] *Feral* means formerly domesticated though now wild.

mountain side. Mention should be made also of the maintenance of a herd of feral park cattle at Vaynol on the border of the National Park. White with black tipped ears, these cattle are dangerous to approach, especially when with calves.

Mountain hares, which turn white in winter, have been introduced into the Park more than once, and both from Scotland and Ireland, and occasional individuals are still reported at intervals, though they have become almost extinct. Brown hares are present in the lowlands, and rabbits, once very numerous, have survived myxomatosis in many places and are showing unmistakable signs of re-establishing themselves. The short tailed field vole, the bank vole and the long tailed field mouse are numerous everywhere, and water voles are present in many places. The dormouse is said to occur in small numbers, though the writer has never observed it. The red squirrel is present in all the wooded areas and is fairly numerous; but the greater part of the Park is free from the grey squirrel, which has reached only to its eastern edge. Amongst the Insectivora, hedgehogs, moles and common shrews are numerous, the latter extending high up the mountains. Lesser shrews, though much less numerous than common shrews, are plentiful and tend to occur in little colonies throughout the region. Water shrews also occur and, although not numerous, are widely distributed. Noctule bats, long eared bats, whiskered bats, pippestrelles, and lesser horseshoe bats occur in the valleys. Daubenton's bat, and Natterer's bat certainly occur and the greater horseshoe bat has been recorded, though the author has not observed these species. Much more information is needed as to the species of bats occurring in the Park and their distribution.

Although the Park is only bounded by the sea for a short distance the coast is nowhere far from its northern and western limits and it is appropriate to mention the numerous breeding colonies of grey seals (Plate IIIb) around Anglesey and Caernarvonshire and the frequent occurrence of various species of whales. Very occasionally some of the larger whalebone whales are stranded, much more often medium size toothed whales, especially the black whale. A few years ago a school of twenty of these, ranging in length from 8 to 20 feet, were stranded in the estuary of the Conway, under the north-east heights of the Park. Porpoises and dolphins are numerous, the latter frequently coming into the Menai Straits and being seen even between the Bridges.

BIRDS

The number of species of birds found in Snowdonia is too great to permit of mention of more than those for which the area is specially notable. Amongst these, pride of place should be given, I think, to the chough. This crow with the orange-red legs and bill and the purple sheen on its glossy black plumage, sometimes called the red-legged jackdaw, is essentially a bird of the high cliffs; a resident that nests in crevices in great rock faces and that loves to display its magnificent powers of flight in the turbulent up-currents of air that characterize precipitous places. Surviving elsewhere in Britain in the sea-cliffs of Cornwall, the Isle of Man, the Hebrides and the west of Ireland, this bird breeds in Snowdonia inland as well as on the northern and western seaboards. Once far more plentiful, it has been holding its own, and even increasing somewhat in numbers, in recent years. There is hope that, with the decline in numbers of gamekeepers and the abolition of the gin trap, the chough once more may become a common bird throughout the mountainous parts of the Park. Another member of the crow family that is much more common is the raven. It breeds on suitable cliffs throughout the Park and can be seen almost everywhere; its deep guttural croak can be heard at a great distance, when the bird is only a speck in the sky. Visitors may hear it often, even in the town of Bangor, passing high overhead, and in the passes or on the mountains it would be hard indeed to overlook it.

The peregrine falcon may be seen in the mountains. It has its aerie on an inaccessible ledge, in just such a place as a raven nests, and it loves to sit on a high rock pinnacle surveying the land below. The female bird or falcon is much larger than the male or tiercel. Common previously, these splendid birds were nearly exterminated during the war because of the destruction they wrought on carrier pigeons used by the armed forces, but now they are gradually regaining their former numbers. Many buzzards, kestrels and a few merlins may be seen also on the mountains. Eagles, however, ceased to breed long ago in Snowdonia, though very rarely a wandering golden eagle may pay a brief visit to the mountains.

Another bird that is characteristic of the highlands, mainly above the 1,000 feet contour, is the ring ouzel. It resembles a blackbird with a white gorget and is a summer visitor, breeding on the mountains and high moorlands. Both red grouse and blackcock are to be seen on the moorlands. Golden plover and dunlin also breed in small numbers on suitable desolate moors. Wherever screes, loose stone walls, or rabbit holes provide nesting sites in the mountains, moors or dunelands, wheatears are to be seen in summer, flaunting their white rumps as they fly from one rock to another.

The valleys of Snowdonia are the haunts of many other birds. Old oak and birch woods are favoured breeding grounds of the pied flycatcher and here, too, redstarts are to be found in summer. Both are strikingly beautiful small birds, about the size of robins, and both build their nests in holes in trees. The male pied flycatcher in summer plumage is black and white, as its name implies. This bird is very local in Britain, breeding freely only in a few chosen places, of which Snowdonia and the Lake District are amongst the principal. The redstart is also local in its occurrence but is more widely distributed. The male bird is brightly coloured, with its white forehead, black throat and orange breast, flanks and rump. The flash of orange which it displays as it takes flight and the curious flirting movement of its tail when perched are characteristic. The mountain torrents running down into the valleys are frequented by dippers and grey wagtails; the young forestry plantations, where the grass is long and rank, by grasshopper warblers. In winter, wild geese of several species visit the coastal saltings and wild swans, both whooper and Bewick's come to many of the lowland lakes. Swimming with their necks held straight up and with lemon yellow patches on the base of their otherwise dark beaks, they are easy to distinguish from the resident mute swans which swim with their necks characteristically curved in an S-bend and whose beaks are red and black with a knob at the base.

REPTILES AND OTHER ANIMALS

Both vipers and grass snakes are numerous in many parts of Snowdonia, and visitors unable to identify them with certainty are well advised to leave them alone. Vipers are harmless creatures unless they are provoked, but their bite is severely poisonous and demands medical treatment with all possible speed. Both snakes are beautiful animals well worth watching at a safe distance of a few yards. The slow worm also occurs commonly and, although snake-like, is really a legless lizard. The little viviparous lizard is very plentiful in many parts of the Park. All these animals are quite harmless, except for the viper, and all are beautiful and interesting creatures worthy of preservation. Strange as it may seem, at least two species of turtles, the leathery turtle and Kemp's loggerhead turtle, have occurred on the adjoining sea coast, though these are very rare visitors to our shores.

Frogs, common toads and palmate newts are plentiful in all suitable habitats and warty newts also are to be found.

Salmon and sewin, or sea trout, ascend all the principal rivers, and brown trout are plentiful. The char or torgoch occurs in Llyn Peris and some other lakes, and the gwyniad is found only in Bala Lake. Sparling or smelts, ascend some of the rivers. Coarse fish are curiously scarce, though perch are plentiful in those lakes in which they do occur, and pike are to be found in Bala and a few other lakes. Lampreys occur in several of the rivers.

Snowdonia is not particularly rich in land or fresh water invertebrate animals; indeed the terrestrial fauna associated with the more acid soils, that cover much of the area, is poor in numbers of species. The highland lakes in the mountain cwms have notably thin faunas and even lowland lakes in the valley bottoms are not rich in animal life. The rivers and lakes are unspoiled by industrial pollution and consequently are particularly favourable for the study of populations almost undisturbed by human intervention. But although in general the area does not support either the variety or the density of population of invertebrate animals that are encountered in, for example, the southern counties of England, it is, nevertheless, one of particular interest in several respects. Representatives of the arctic-alpine fauna are to be found, as for instance the little planarian worm, *Planaria alpina*, which occurs in the streams and is a relic of the Ice Age. It is a region where the characteristically northern and southern faunas overlap. Another feature of interest is the changes in the fauna which are resulting from extensive afforestation, with the consequent increase in forest insects. The marine invertebrate fauna of the shores adjoining the Park is in striking contrast, being particularly rich and varied, especially in the Menai Straits.

The Nature Conservancy is the statutory body charged with the preservation of the fauna, flora and geological monuments of Britain. Its Welsh headquarters is situated at Bangor and it maintains a number of reserves within the Park, of which the principal are Llyn Idwal (Plate IX) and its surroundings, the summit of Cader Idris and Tremadoc Wood. Research work on the fauna of the Park is undertaken by the staff of the Nature Conservancy. Other research centres in the area, concerned with the fauna, are the Departments of Zoology and of Agricultural Zoology of the University College of North Wales at Bangor, the Marine Biological Station of the University of Wales at Menai Bridge and the Department of Zoology of the University College of Wales at Aberystwyth. There is also a Field Station and Observatory, devoted largely to ornithology, maintained on Bardsey Island.

4

Principal Antiquities within the Park

LATE STONE OR EARLY BRONZE AGE

THERE are many remains of the *long barrow* and, what appears to have been its immediate successor, the *great round barrow* in Wales, but only a few within the Park boundary. When complete with their covering-mounds (generally of loose stones rather than earth), they are, or were, called *carneddau* (sing. *carnedd*). In the ruined state where one or more burial chambers are exposed to view, looking like massive stone tables, they are called *cromlechau* (sing. *cromlech*) (Plate IV). Earlier antiquaries believed them to be sacrificial altars of the Druids. That they were all tombs of the Neolithic or Early Bronze Age people has now been clearly shown, though the Druids, arriving more than a thousand years later with the Iron Age Celt, would doubtless regard them as venerable and sacred objects and very likely make use of any one which had lost its covering in the manner supposed. See pages 65, 84.

THE LATER BRONZE AGE

The tomb is a much smaller round barrow, also called *carnedd*, containing a smaller and more box-like burial-chamber called *cist* or *cistfaen* (stone chest). These are numerous throughout the area. Nearly all the principal summits are surmounted by a cairn which appears to have been sepulchral and of this period.

The *stone circle* is rare. See page 63. The small circle which is really only the exposed curb of a round barrow that has disappeared, is fairly common and should not be confounded with the larger free-standing circle.

The solitary monolith, *maen hir* (plu. *meini hirion*), which may be a single grave-stone or the relic of a circle, is not common either. See page 62.

THE IRON AGE (CELTIC PEOPLES)

The principal relic of this Age is the *hut-circle*, that is, the foundation of a beehive-shaped dwelling. These occur singly or in groups on high ground in many parts of the Park, but most abundantly in the north and west and on the western slopes of the Rhinogs. See pages 63, 84.

Arrow-stones. See page 63.

Boiling-mounds.

These are kidney- or crescent-shaped mounds always found near a stream and with the concave side facing it. They are associated with stones reddened by fire and much charcoal. The recessed side of the mound has a hearth, which seems to indicate clearly that these places were communal kitchens, though they are generally found in places apart from hut-circle communities, which suggests that their users were nomads of a later time which have left no other trace. Like the Assiniboin Indians of North America they boiled water by plunging red-hot stones into it instead of placing the vessel on the fire.

Hill-forts.

Most of these are marked with a conventional sign on the sketch-maps. Of particular interest is the one above Llanbedr-y-cennin, called Pen-y-Gaer. At its weakest approach, on the south side, a quantity of pointed stones have been fixed upright in the ground to deter the onrush of an attacker. The same type of defence is found on the west coast of Ireland but not elsewhere in Wales, a forerunner of the mediaeval *chevaux de frise* and the modern tank-trap. See page 61.

ROMAN REMAINS

There are three forts of the *castellum* or road-station type within the Park boundary with clearly marked ramparts; Caer Llugwy page 63, Tomen-y-mur page 91, and Caer Gai page 89. There were similar forts at Pennal and Dolgelley. Of the former there is little to be seen, of the latter none at all. The modern highway from Bala Lake to Dolgelley closely follows the Roman road from Caer Gai, of which one or two remains can be made out plainly. A *marching-camp*, or temporary fortification, has been identified at Pen-y-Gwryd page 69.

REMAINS OF THE EARLY CHRISTIAN CHURCH OF BRITAIN

Inscribed stones of the fifth, sixth, and seventh centuries A.D. page 54 and Plate V, a & b. The Welsh *parish church* page 54 and Plate V c.

WELSH CASTLES

Those built before the English conquest of 1283 (of the motte-and-bailey type) were copies of the Norman model. Later stone castles show one or two slightly distinctive features, the chief being a square tower with one side apse-shaped. An example of this is at Castell-y-Bere. Of the high *motte-mound* made to carry a wooden tower there is a large specimen in Bala town, and a smaller one a mile away on the far side of the lake. Another is at a farm in Dolbenmaen only a few yards beyond the Park boundary, which runs on the opposite (north) side of the road. The foundations of a stone keep are at Dinas Emrys page 75 and Castell Carn Dochan page 89, and one complete at Dolwyddelan page 81. Castell-y-Bere as remodelled represents the more advanced type of English castle of the thirteenth century, page 95.

ENGLISH CASTLES

There are only two; the motte-mound constructed by William Rufus within the enclosure of the old Roman fort at Tomen-y-mur, page 91, and the great Edwardian fortress at Harlech, page 85 and Plate VI.

HOUSES

To enumerate the old houses in the Park, once owned by Welsh families who had lived on their lands in many cases from the time of the native Princes, is quite beyond the scope of this Guide. Many go back to the sixteenth century, replacing earlier ones on the same site. They are simple buildings often constructed with enormous stones for which the Welsh seem to have inherited a megalithic aptitude for moving and raising, as is also seen in the clapper-bridges. Plate VII (*b*).

In the mountains, the farm-house in the valley bottom was supplemented by another on the higher ground, called *hafod*, where the family migrated with their animals to the summer pasture. The ruins of these, still seen in so many places, date mainly from the early eigthteenth century, and before the Enclosure Acts.

HORSE-STEPS

To make it easier for pack-horses to cross the higher mountain passes and gain access to other steeply situated places the track was paved and curbed with large rough stones and had steps made at suitable intervals according to the gradient. There are only a few remains of these, the most notable being the Roman Steps at Cwm Bychan (Plate XV and page 86). There is a fair sample in the upper part of the mediaeval road through Nant Ffrancon—below the Telford turnpike-road. Another relic is noted on page 64. The typical *sarn* was formed by placing large slates, usually end-to-end, forming a dry-shod path. A perfect example is the old path connecting Talsarnau (Over the Sarns) with the parish church at Llanfihangel-y-traethau. Beside the road from Capel Curig to Pen-y-Gwryd (turnpiked in 1805) can still

PLATE IV (a). Capel Garmon Cromlech

PLATE IV (b). Maen-y-bardd Cromlech

PLATE V (a)   PLATE V (b)

Early Christian monuments, Penmachno
(*See page iv note for the inscriptions and translations*)

PLATE V (c). Llanrhychwyn Church. The small bell-cote and aisles
under separate roofs are typical of the old Welsh parish church

PLATE VI. The Gate-house, Harlech Castle, late thirteenth century

PLATE VII (b). Entrance doorway, Gilar, typical Welsh cyclopean construction

PLATE VII (a). The Gate-house, Gilar, dated 1623

be seen the huge slate slabs which formed the old pack-horse sarn. They are now set up on edge against the bank.

DRY-STONE WALLS

These are a great feature of the Park, and vary between those made of the rough flattish stones in the Caernarvonshire mountains and the smooth rounded stones on the Merioneth coast and western slopes of the Rhinogs. As they are never likely to be repeated, an interest in their skill of construction and their pleasant appearance will grow with the course of time. The *slate-fence* of the nineteenth century (now also being rapidly replaced by barbed wire and concrete) made a charming addition to the landscape and what may remain will soon come to be prized.

On the lower slopes of the mountains the old boundary walls of the farms can be traced by great stones embedded in low banks which take a snake-like course along the slope. They represent an old irregular frontier of conquest where bit by bit of the rough mountain has been brought into cultivation or pasture (each new bit called a *ffridd*). They belong to the days before sheep farming in the mountains had replaced goat-keeping, and were abandoned when the Enclosure Acts enabled the big landowner to build the high dry-stone walls in the upper mountain, often on the watershed itself.

5

Mountaineering

by CHARLES EVANS

ALTHOUGH there are many outlying crags and ridges scattered throughout north and central Wales, the best mountaineering is to be found in the four mountain groups of Caernarvonshire: the Carnedd range, Tryfan and the range of the Glyder, Snowdon, and those mountains which lie west of Rhyd-ddu.

Eryri has a character which the mountaineer recognizes at once as akin to that of higher ranges, and so climbers often describe its mountains as 'real mountains': the landscape is bare and rugged; the traces of the work of ice are everywhere to be seen; some of the tops, which are often sharp, can only be reached and traversed by ways that are steep and rough; many of the ridges are rocky and broken, and give a sense of height because the slopes fall steeply from them on either side, and some of the high ground, when transformed in winter by snow, may be safely accessible only to experienced and properly equipped mountaineers.

In Wales the development of mountaineering as a sport followed rather slowly the growth of the custom of walking for health and pleasure. By the middle of the nineteenth century to walk up Snowdon was a popular excursion, but it was not until towards the end of the century that climbing as we know it began: English climbers, among them some who were pioneers of Alpine mountaineering, had already found in Wales, crags and ridges on which they could practise for their summer climbing; now they also found there a kind of climbing worth doing for its own sake. Among these was C. E. Matthews who had, in 1870, founded the 'Society of Welsh Rabbits', an informal group of Alpinists who came each winter to stay at Pen-y-Gwryd. In 1898 the Climbers' Club was founded, with Matthews as its first president, a club which ever since has had a profound influence on climbing in Wales.

About the turn of the century several pioneer climbing groups were active in Wales: J. M. Archer Thomson and his friends, local men, were quietly exploring Tryfan, the ranges of the Carnedd, the Glyder, and Lliwedd; Owen Glynne Jones, the Abraham brothers, A. W. Andrews, and Steeple and Barlow were some of the gifted explorers who were finding new routes at almost every visit; and, rather later, Winthrop Young began the custom, which continued until the outbreak of the second World War, of holding parties each Easter at Pen-y-Pass, at which young climbers, most of them then from the older universities, were made welcome. After the first World War, at the instigation of Herbert Carr, the Climbers' Club bought an old cottage called Helyg, and turned it into the first successful climbing 'hut' in the country. It was the beginning of a new era: Helyg, and many other huts like it, established by various clubs in the last thirty years, have given cheap and simple accommodation to the young men who used them as bases for the more intense exploration of the crags of the district. New parts of the old cliffs were explored, and hitherto unclimbed cliffs were visited and at last climbed. New climbs of a more serious character than the old routes began to be a part of the ordinary repertoire of the best climbers: climbs on such steep facets as Tryfan's Terrace Wall, and Idwal's Holly Tree Wall; climbs on neglected and grassy cliffs like those about the Devil's Kitchen, a few climbs on the steep rocks flanking the Llanberis Pass, notably Dinas Mot; and most important of all, climbs on the two main buttresses of Clogwyn du'r Arddu. The new pioneers were many, but two names stand out: Colin Kirkus and Menlove Edwards.

By 1939 it might have been thought that the limit of what was possible had been reached, but it was not so. The Mountain Training Wings during the war, Peter Harding's explorations after the war, when he was writing a guide-book to the Llanberis Pass and to Clogwyn-du'r-Arddu, and the new climbs made by Joe Brown and the other members of the Manchester Rock and Ice Club have shown that it will never be safe to say of our rocks that all that man can do on them has now been done.

Within the Park there are mountain-walking expeditions which it would be hard to beat anywhere—the traverses, for instance, of the main summits in each district: of Cader Idris from Arthog over Tyrau Mawr to Tal-y-Llyn or the Cross Foxes; of the ridge of the Aran from Dinas Mawddwy to Llanuwchllyn; and of the range of the Carneddau from Tal-y-Fan to Ogwen—but what is peculiar to Wales is a first-class supply of the kind of expedition that comes between a walk and a real climb. Of these scrambles, three are outstanding: the traverse of the ridge that runs from Y Garn, near Rhyd Ddu, over Mynydd Drws-y-Coed, Trum-y-Ddisgl, Tal-y-Mignedd, and Craig Cwm Silyn to Garnedd Gôch; the traverse of Tryfan by the north and south ridges, followed by the ascent of the Bristly ridge to Glyder Fach, and the descent of the Gribin ridge; and the Horseshoe of Snowdon. The Horseshoe can be varied in many ways: I think it is best started from the Crib Gôch end, so as not to have to climb the screes from Bwlch-y-Saethau to the top of Snowdon; Crib Gôch itself can be reached either by its straightforward north ridge that rises from above Dinas Mot, or by the more usual and slightly harder ridge from Bwlch Môch; from Bwlch-y-Saethau the Horseshoe can be followed over the rocky and grassy crest of Lliwedd, or left for the descent, to Glaslyn, of the easy Gribin ridge; climbers can take in the Horseshoe to round off a climb on Lliwedd or on the cliffs above Cwm Glas; and scramblers who know a bit about rock-climbing and about the use of a rope can tackle, as a way of joining the Horseshoe, the climb up the ridge behind the Parson's Nose. This is definitely a climb, but a very easy one; it starts up either the nose itself, a 'Moderately Difficult' climb, or more easily up one of the gullies behind the nose, and continues as a series of steep steps separated by piled boulders; the ridge narrows as it rises, and becomes easier, until suddenly the crest of Crib-y-Ddisgl is reached and the whole panorama of the Horseshoe comes into view. In winter, covered with ice and snow, this ridge, and the traverse after it of the main ridge of the Horseshoe northwards over Crib Gôch, can be an exacting expedition.

Rock-climbing in the National Park is of all kinds: there are large areas suitable for beginners; and there are some of the finest crags for experts in the country—huge, steep and smooth; but the distinctive Welsh climb, of which we are lucky to have several, and which is of a type not easily come by in British hills, is the long and continuous route, not necessarily hard, which calls for some ability to find the way and for some knowledge of bad rock, and takes the climber to the top of a mountain; on this sort of climb the climber feels that he is taking, at least for the moment, the easiest way; it is what he calls 'the good non-artificial mountaineering route'.

The climbing is grouped around two centres, at one or other of which most climbers stay: the Nant Ffrancon Pass, and the Llanberis Pass. Ogwen Cottage in the old days, the farms in the Ogwen valley, and later the 'huts', Helyg, Tal-y-braich, Glan Dena and the Youth Hostel at Idwal, have all had their devotees, and the Ogwen valley, though it may not have the best or the hardest climbs, has a variety of routes of a quality which ensures a steady stream of visiting climbers. It is one of the best of starting grounds: on the Milestone Buttress, on the east face of Tryfan, on Glyder Fach (Plate VIII), on the Gribin Facet, and on Idwal Slabs, are climbs on perfect rock where the beginner can be shown in benign surroundings the elements of technique and of rope management. For those who are already climbers there is here a good selection of old favourites, climbs of about 'Very Difficult' standard, fine routes in themselves which, though many of them were first climbed fifty years ago, still give year by year pleasure to those who like what climbers call a 'mountaineering route': on Tryfan, the Gashed Crag route and the Grooved Arete; on Glyder Fach, the Direct route; on the Devil's Kitchen cliffs, the Devil's Staircase; on Craig-yr-Ysfa, Amphitheatre Buttress and the Great Gully; and on Ysgolion Duon in Cwm Llafar, the Western Gully. Of the hardest and most exposed modern routes there are not many in the district, and they are scattered, some on small steep facets of the larger crags, Terrace Wall and Holly Tree Wall; some on gully walls, the Munich climb, Advocate's Wall, and the climbs which overlook the Amphi-theatre of Craig-yr-Ysfa; and one or two on isolated crags, such as the Central route on Llech Du. There are at present three Climbers' Club guide-books to the area: one is for Tryfan and the Glyder, one for Cwm Idwal, and one for the range of the Carneddau.

The popularity of the Llanberis Pass as a centre has been less continuous than that of Nant Ffrancon in spite of the fact that from it most of the finest and hardest of Welsh climbs can easily be reached. Here, except for the Parson's Nose, and one or two such climbs as Slanting Buttress on Lliwedd, there is little that is suitable for absolute beginners; but for climbers of moderate ability and experience there is a bewildering amount and variety of climbing.

Lliwedd, in Cwm Dyli, has a volume of the Climbers' Club guide-books to itself. It is one of the largest and most imposing of Welsh crags, criss-crossed with routes of all standards of difficulty. Its characteristic climbs are long, of medium difficulty, running from the foot to the top of the east peak; on them the route is not always simple to find and the rock is sometimes unsound, and the climber new to the crag tastes the feeling of finding his way up the face of a big mountain.

High in Cwm Glas are two cliffs on which are a number of good 'Very Difficult' climbs: Crib Gôch Buttress, on which is the fine Reade's Route; and Clogwyn-y-Ddisgl, on which are several steep climbs on rough sound rock, of which the most popular are the Gambit and the Rectory Chimneys.

But the resident in the pass need not go even so far as this for his climbing: within a few minutes' walk of the road are some of the hardest and steepest climbs in the country. South of the road is the smooth grey outcrop of Dinas Mot; north of the road, and immediately over-looking it, are 'The Three Cliffs', Dinas Cromlech, Carreg Wastad, and Clogwyn-y-Crochan; and only a little farther, on the way up Cwm Glas, is the forbidding buttress of Cyrn Las. On all these there are routes of the highest quality, exposed, difficult, on good rock, where the most skilful rock-climbers can find all they want when bad weather, or lack of inclination, prevents them from visiting their Mecca, Clogwyn-du'r-Arddu, in Cwm Brwynog.

'Cloggy', as it is familiarly called, is most easily reached by walking up the Snowdon track from Llanberis village. Its main buttresses were not climbed until 1927 and 1928, but now each has on it a number of routes on which great difficulty, and long distances between resting places, are combined with tremendous exposure. Here, during the last thirty years, sheer walls and steep slabs, where then only a single doubtful possibility of a route could be seen, have been transformed into a playground on which at least one climb is made up by joining in a girdle traverse the hardest sections of all the existing more conventional routes.

For all but a few climbers, these are climbs for summer time and good weather. In winter most climbers in Wales prefer a different sort of expedition. Snow which has fallen heavily and packed hard, ice formed from the melting and re-freezing of the snow, and rime which gathers on the rocks of the summit ridges, alter in winter the upper slopes of our mountains to a degree which makes them to the summer visitor almost unrecognizable. Then, when the more usual rock-climbs are impossible, some of the high gullies and ridges can give first-class sport. It is a chancy sport, which depends entirely on the weather; an expedition may one day be exacting and exhilarating, which on the next, through a change of temperature, is laborious and dull. The best conditions are found in clear frosty weather, some time after a period of heavy snowfall, and the best places are the north-facing Clogwyn-y-Garnedd of Snowdon, the north-facing hollows of the Glyder, and the gullies of Ysgolion Duon, in Cwm Llafar.

It must be plain from this short survey that in a hundred years mountaineering in Wales has changed out of all recognition: the least accessible secrets of the hills would seem now to have been laid bare, and solitude even in their remotest recesses become impossible to find. It is not so: climbers are gregarious folk, and, like other men, imitative, and a man need only go to Wales in winter, and at mid-week, and seek ways a little off the beaten track, to find these mountains as mysterious and solitary, and, for him, as unexplored, as they were in the days of the pioneers.

6

Country-going and Communications

by REG. TAYLOR

THERE are many interests that are no more than adjuncts to the more generalized and perhaps mystical appeal which the country has for many people. Even in the days when the country lay more easily at one's doorstep the appeal was there; but now, when we live within ever widening circles of industrialism, there has developed an almost explosive urge to escape occasionally to a more natural environment. This urge has given rise to a widespread outdoor movement; to many movements, for one man's way of going about is not necessarily to another man's liking: to country-going, in fact, as we understand it today.

Walking and cycling are the simplest and most popular ways of country-going, and of the number of organizations that promote outdoor activities of this type within the National Park, perhaps the most widely known is the *Youth Hostels Association*, which interprets even the word Youth in a liberal manner, and demands little more of its members than that they should behave as civilized and responsible people when roaming the countryside. In return, it offers simple but attractive accommodation at various points within the Park. The addresses of these hostels, together with those of other organizations mentioned in this chapter, are listed at pages 37-40. It is no coincidence that one of the first networks of hostels should have been developed in Wales in what is now the National Park, and it is our purpose here to note their usefulness for those who like this relatively casual way of travel.

Little advice need be offered to cyclists: they may, within reason, travel how they will and where they will; even to the uttermost parts of the hills if their agility permits. Walkers must plan more expeditiously, either to travel on foot directly from hostel to hostel, or to integrate their travels with the movements of public transport within the Park.

Railway routes are useful but limited: no trains, for example, run on Sundays. Nevertheless there are four lines that can be helpful on other days. One runs west from Bala through Dolgelley to Barmouth, then north to Bangor or south to Aberdovey. It is useful for anyone wishing to walk or climb on the Arans, or Cader Idris, or the coastal range of hills behind Harlech. The second line runs from Bala to

33

Ffestiniog and serves the Arenigs and the high moors of the Migneint, as well as the most attractive country around Ffestiniog itself. The third line hugs the north-easterly fringe of the Park from Llandudno to Betws-y-Coed, continuing through the Park, along the Lledr valley and under the watershed to Ffestiniog. By planning one's routes according to the running of the trains much ground can be covered that might otherwise be missed. The fourth skirts the northern boundary of the Park, from Conway to Bangor. This is the main Chester to Holyhead line, but from points along it one may foray by bus into the Park.

Three other railways must be mentioned, particularly on account of their local interest. They are narrow gauge railways, two of which have been saved from extinction by enthusiasts, who have repaired and now maintain the track and rolling stock, and run the trains as holiday attractions during the summer months. One is the Talyllyn Railway (Plate XVII b) that climbs from Towyn into the hills behind. Its name is misleading, for the line finishes at Abergynolwyn, some five miles short of Tal-y-Llyn (page 95). The second is the Festiniog Railway which all but disappeared a few years ago but is fighting its way back up the Vale of Ffestiniog from Portmadoc as volunteer railwaymen repair and relay the track. Both of these railways use engines and rolling stock built in the 1860's. The third is the Snowdon Mountain Railway which takes thousands of visitors yearly up the mountain from Llanberis.

A more comprehensive system of transport is provided by Crosville Motor Services whose buses operate on all the main roads throughout North Wales and most of the winding byeways to remote settlements up in the hills. Their timetable No. 5 covers the whole of the Park area. It is available at all their depots or by post from their head office at Crane Wharf, Chester. They also serve the district by express coaches from Liverpool. Purple Motors run local services from Bangor and Whiteway Motors from Caernarvon. They go as far as Portmadoc via Cwellyn Lake and Snowdon Ranger Youth Hostel and operate all the year round (Crosville serves this route in the summer only).

There is another way of going about, provided by the *Holiday Fellowship* and the *Co-operative Holidays Association*, who have a number of guest houses within the Park. This way is for those who like a more settled and gregarious mode of country travel. Here at one or other of the guest houses one becomes part of a community for a week or a fortnight. The country-going is finely planned and carefully graded so that one may be tough or not-so-tough according to temperament or capabilities. The Holiday Fellowship also organizes walking tours in co-operation with the Y.H.A. for those who wish to cover more ground than is possible from a fixed base, but still in settled company.

PLATE VIII. Climbing on Glyder Fach

PLATE IX. Cwm Idwal, looking towards 'Idwal Slabs' on Giyder Fawr

There is yet a third way of going about which is for newcomers to country-going. In this connection one naturally thinks first of youngsters for whom some guidance is advisable if they are to develop a sober appreciation of the countryside between fits of youthful exuberance; and the Y.H.A., H.F. and C.H.A. in their several ways encourage and provide special facilities for school parties or other juvenile parties that wish either to undertake field work in the Park, or merely to broaden their knowledge of it. For those of maturer years there are occasional hillcraft courses run by the Y.H.A., but much more comprehensive training in mountain and other outdoor activity is provided by the *Central Council of Physical Recreation* at its centre at Plas-y-Brenin, Capel Curig. Here in all seasons one can acquire country lore and train in all the arts of mountain craft, mobile camping and canoeing, to which pony-trekking may soon be added; and in due season there is ski-ing and snow work. The normal course at the centre lasts a week, but additional short weekend courses are also arranged. Other courses of varying length are run in co-operation with other authorities, and of these the girls' Outward Bound course referred to in the following paragraph is an example.

Outward Bound courses are for the hardy and they are organized as a challenge to the will and initiative of young people. Courses for boys are run at the Outward Bound School at Aberdovey, and for girls at Plas-y-Brenin, Capel Curig. The spirit of adventure is latent in most young people but for relatively few is there opportunity to find outlet for it in expeditions to the Antarctic or the Himalayas. The courses are planned to show that adventure is basically a test of character and stamina, and that one need not go so far afield to find it. The boys' course at Aberdovey, as may be imagined, has a nautical tang and reaches its climax in a short sea voyage in a small sailing ship, but it includes some cross-country work in which the boys cover up to 35 miles in a day over country that rises in places to 3,000 feet. The girls' course at Capel Curig is more varied and rather less rigorous. Life afloat is limited to canoes and to the inland waters of the twin lakes of Mymbyr, but life ashore includes both rock-climbing and mobile camping. Both boys' and girls' courses last approximately one month.

Camping has a venerable history of association with nomadic movement, but it is only in comparatively modern times that the tang of adventure pervading it has been discerned and exploited. By no other means can one really get to the heart of the country. Even the approach to a farmer for permission to camp can help to break the traditional reserve between townsman and countryman. Campers are pre-eminently people who like to travel casually. There is an organizing body, the Camping Club of Great Britain and Ireland, but there is no

organized camping within the National Park, apart from one attractive
Forestry Commission site at Hafod Ruffyd Isaf, Beddgelert. All that is
expected of campers is that when they move on they will leave no more
than a patch of yellowed grass to show where they have been.

Caravaning also has nomadic roots. We associate it with woodland
glades but find it more often now in main road lay-byes. Like camping,
it confers freedom of movement but this is not exploited so widely
within the National Park as it could be. Caravaners are more gregarious
than campers and tend to cluster in known sites. The Caravan Club of
Great Britain and Ireland has done much to organize such sites on a
suitable basis. There are a number available within the Park, including
that of the Forestry Commission at Beddgelert. This particular site
comes near to the ideal which would be welcomed throughout the
National Park, being well-laid out, secluded, screened by woodlands
and offering adequate facilities.

Fishing. Everywhere in the Park there are mountain streams and lakes
inhabited by trout. The streams are exceedingly clear and often do not
colour even in a heavy flood. They are also rapid, with swift runs into
pool after pool, and the wet fly can be fished successfully. Wales remains
a stronghold of this art—which is not to say that the dry-fly man might
not make a heavier basket on occasions and in particular places. Worm
fishing is not generally frowned on and, for this purpose, the two hook
Pennel tackle, weighted with only one small shot, is best.

There is a great deal of free fishing for small trout in the mountains
(though the local conservancy may make a small charge for a rod licence).
In the larger rivers, stretches of water are preserved by angling associations or water boards who issue tickets for the day or longer. Salmon
and sea-trout (sewin) run up many rivers. In the Ogwen they reach
spawning-grounds over six hundred feet above sea level.

Coarse fish are as rare as trout are in the Midlands, though there is
a wide variety in Bala Lake (where pike can make a good living and grow
heavy). Here the uncommon gwyniad is found—a member of the salmon
family and cousin to the pollan of Lough Neagh—but he is seldom
drawn from the water except in a net.

For all those who would like to be out and about within the Park
there is an organization of one sort or another that can help them do
so according to their fancy. And for walkers there is a network of public
communications reaching to the hinterlands of the Park, ready to help
them on their way at the beginning of the day and to rescue them at its
end.

Some Useful Addresses

ANGLING ASSOCIATIONS

Bala Angling Association, Elmdon, Bro Eryl, Bala.

Cambrian Angling Association, 75, Manod Street, Blaenau Ffestiniog.

Dolgelley Angling Association, Bodlondeb, Dolgelley.

Prysor Angling Association, Glasfryn, Trawsfynydd.

River Artro Fishing Association, Islwyn, Bryndeiliog, Llanbedr.

The New Dovey Fishery Association (1929), Ltd., Cambrian House, Machynlleth.

Ystumaner Angling Association, 14 Water Street, Abergynolwyn.

Conway Fishing Association, Gwydyr Hotel, Betws-y-Coed.

The Conway Fishery Consultative Committee, 36, Station Road, Llanrwst.

Criccieth and Llanystumdwy Angling Association, Arncliffe, Queen's Road, Criccieth.

Dolgarrog Fishing Club, 3, Tayler Avenue, Dolgarrog.

The Dolwyddelan Fishing Association, 10, Maes y Braich, Dolwyddelan.

Glaslyn Angling Association, 5, Britannia Terrace, Portmadoc.

The Llanrwst Anglers' Club, 36, Station Road, Llanrwst.

Ogwen Valley Angling Association, 42, Water Street, Llanllechid, Nr. Bangor.

Pennant Angling Association, 1, Marda Cottages, Tremadoc.

Penrhyn Fishing Club, 35, Friars Road, Bangor, Caernarvonshire.

Pwllheli and District Angling Association, 3, Ship Terrace, Abererch, Pwllheli.

The Seiont, Gwyrfai and Llyfni Anglers' Society, Paris House, 17, Marcus Street, Caernarvon.

Ysbytty Ifan Angling Association, Yspyty Vicarage, Betws-y-Coed.

ARCHAEOLOGICAL AND HISTORICAL SOCIETIES

Caernarvonshire Historical Society
Hon. Secretary: Mr. J. E. Owen-Jones, Bryn Eirias, Priestley Road, Caernarvon.
Hon. Secretary (Archaeological Branch): Mr. C. A. Gresham, Bryn-y-Deryn, Criccieth.

Cambrian Archaeological Association
Hon. Secretary: Mr. H. Noel Jerman, 103, Heathwood Road, Cardiff.

Merioneth Historical and Record Society
Hon. Secretary: Mr. B. Maelor Jones, Education Dept., County Offices, Dolgelley.

BOATING AND YACHTING CLUBS

Bala Boating and Yachting Club, Bala.
Dovey Sailing Club, Celtic House, Aberdovey.
Merioneth Yacht Club, The Quay, Barmouth.

THE CAMPING CLUB OF GREAT BRITAIN AND IRELAND

Headquarters: 35, Old Kent Road, London, S.E.1.

THE CARAVAN CLUB OF GREAT BRITAIN AND IRELAND

Headquarters: New Oxford House, Bloomsbury Way, London, W.C.1.

THE CENTRAL COUNCIL OF PHYSICAL RECREATION

Headquarters: 6, Bedford Square, London, W.C.1.
Centre: Plas-y-Brenin, Capel Curig.

THE CO-OPERATIVE HOLIDAYS ASSOCIATION

Headquarters: Birch Heys, Cromwell Range, Manchester 14.
Centres: Orielton Hall, Barmouth; Plas Heulog, Llanfairfechan; Lledr Hall, Pont-y-pant.

COUNCIL FOR THE PRESERVATION OF RURAL WALES

Merioneth Branch
Hon. Secretary: Mrs. K. O. Rees, Cefnydd, Dolgelley.
Caernarvonshire Branch
Hon. Secretary: Mr. W. Twiston Davies, Bron Hebog, Beddgelert.

THE HOLIDAY FELLOWSHIP LIMITED

Headquarters: 142, Great North Way, Hendon, London, N.W.4.
Centres: Bryn Corach, Conway; Bryn Dinas, Nant Gwynant; Trem Enlli, Towyn.

MOUNTAIN RESCUE POSTS

Mountain Rescue Committee
North Wales Organizer: Mr. C. B. Briggs, Pen-y-Gwrhyd Hotel, Nr. Llanberis.
Posts
Cwellyn Arms Hotel, Rhyd Ddu: Tel. Beddgelert 267.
Idwal Cottage Youth Hostel: Public Tel. Box by hostel. L.O.G. Ogwen 1
Ogwen Cottage: Tel. Bethesda 211.
The Outward Bound Sea School, Aberdovey: Tel. Aberdovey 105.
Pen-y-Gwrhyd Hotel: Tel. Llanberis 211.
Other Posts
The Fire Station, Dolgelley: Tel. Police, Dolgelley.
Kings Youth Hostel, nr. Dolgelley.
Rescue Team
R.A.F. Mountain Rescue Team, Valley, Holyhead: Tel. through Police.

MOUNTAINEERING

Member Clubs of the British Mountaineering Council which have headquarters or huts in North Wales

Cave & Crag Club. Hon Secretary: D. D. Snell, 29, Beacon Road, Wylde Green, Sutton Coldfield.

Chester Mountaineering Club. Hon. Secretary: Miss M. Thomas, 4, Victoria Pathway, Queen's Park, Chester.

Climbers' Club. Hon. Secretary: A. Blackshaw, 114, Cambridge Street, Warwick Square, London, S.W.1.

Manchester University Mountaineering Club. Hon. Secretary: The Mountaineering Club, c/o The University Union, Burlington Street, Manchester 15.

Midland Association of Mountaineers. Hon. Secretary: A. H. Robinson, Lansdowne, Knowle, Solihull, Warwicks.

Mountain Club. Hon. Secretary: Miss Jean Turner, 83, Wolverhampton Road, Stafford.

Mountaineering Club of North Wales. Hon. Secretary: R. Lloyd Roberts, 14, Ogwen Terrace, Bethesda, North Wales.

Oread Mountaineering Club. Hon. Secretary: L. Hatchett, 598, Burton Road, Littleover, Derby.

Pinnacle Club. Hon. Secretary: Mrs. S. Long, 28, West Shrubbery, Redland, Bristol 6.

Rucksack Club. Hon. Secretary: J. E. Byrom, Highfield, 3, Douglas Road, Hazel Grove, Stockport.

University College of North Wales Mountaineering Club. Hon. Secretary: The Mountaineering Club, c/o University Union, University College, Bangor.

Vagabond Mountaineering Club. Hon. Secretary: B. A. Mnew, 554, Mather Avenue, Liverpool 19.

Guides Holding the British Mountaineering Council Certificate

Mountain Guides
T. W. Campion, Nyth Bran, Capel Curig, North Wales.
Gwen Moffatt, Maen-y-Bardd, Ro Wen, Nr. Conway, North Wales.
J. R. Lees c/o Mountain Rescue Section, R.A.F. Valley, Anglesey, North Wales.
S. Styles, Borth-y-Gest, Portmadoc, North Wales.

Rock Climbing Guides
G. Dwyer, Tal-y-Waen, Capel Curig, North Wales.
Gwen Moffatt, Maen-y-Bardd, Ro Wen, Nr. Conway, North Wales.
J. R. Lees, c/o Mountain Rescue Section, R.A.F. Valley, Anglesey, North Wales.
G. J. Sutton, 1, Pembroke Road, Clifton, Bristol.

THE NATURE CONSERVANCY

Regional Office: Y Fron, The Crescent, Upper Bangor, Bangor, Caernarvonshire.

THE OUTWARD BOUND TRUST

Headquarters: 123, Victoria Street, Westminster, London, S.W.1.

Centre: The Outward Bound Sea School, Aberdovey.

THE RAMBLERS' ASSOCIATION

Headquarters: 48, Park Road, Baker Street, London, N.W.1.

Liverpool District and North Wales Area Office. Hon. Secretary: Mr. E. W. Crane, 13, Hazelhurst Road, Liverpool 4.

SNOWDONIA PARK JOINT ADVISORY COMMITTEE

County Offices, Penarlag, Dolgelley, Merioneth.

THE YOUTH HOSTELS ASSOCIATION

Headquarters: Trevelyan House, St. Albans, Herts.

Merseyside Regional Office (for Snowdonia). Secretary: Mr. T. E. Fairclough, 93a, Scotland Road, Liverpool 3.

Hostels

Idwal Cottage, Lake Ogwen. (G.R. 649604[1])

Bryn Hall, Llanllechid. (G.R. 633694)

Rhiw Farm, Ro Wen. (G.R. 746721)

Oaklands, Nr. Llanrwst. (G.R. 812585)

Plas Curig, Capel Curig. (G.R. 725579)

Llanberis. (G.R. 574597)

Snowdon Ranger, Rhyd Ddu. (G.R. 564551)

Bryn Gwynant, Nant Gwynant (G.R. 640513)

Lledr House, Pont-y-Pant. (G.R. 749535)

Cae'rblaidd, Ffestiniog. (G.R. 705428)

Pen-y-Garth, Harlech. (G.R. 581308)

Pont ar Eden, Ganllwyd. (G.R. 735266)

Kings, Nr. Dolgelley. (G.R. 684161)

Plas Rhiwaedog, Bala. (G.R. 947348)

---

[1] Grid Reference.

A Topographical Description
of the Park

THE MAPS

The maps following this page have been specially prepared for the Guide by Mr. G. S. Holland assisted by Miss Joan Emerson. They give all locations mentioned in the text either by name or one of the conventional signs given below. The area has been divided into five sections as shown on the key-map (1) which also indicates clearly the boundary of the Park. Things likely to be of particular interest are noted by ringed numbers with their references on each map.

The Editor would like to thank the cartographers for the great care and trouble they have taken in preparing these maps—with such excellent results in clarity and art.

Key

Snowdonia National Park Boundary ▬ ▬ ▬ ▬	County boundary ▬·▬·▬·▬·
Place of interest .... ⑦	Highest point .... ▲
Old church ....,........,........ ✚	Roman fort ....,...... ⊓
Modern church .... +	Iron Age fort .....,......⊙
Main road ....≃≃ ══	Cromlech .... ⌐
Minor road ...., ========	Motte-mound ..,........,....Δ
Path.......................... --------	Standing stone ....⊥
Roman road or ancient trackway	Early Church Monument . X
Railway .... +++++++	Farm or house................ ■
Narrow-gauge railway........... +++++++	Youth Hostel ....Ⓨ
National Trust property..........(NT)	Nature Reserve............NR

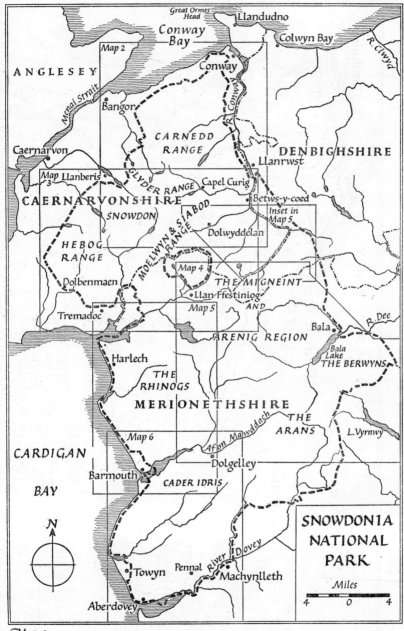

Map 1

43

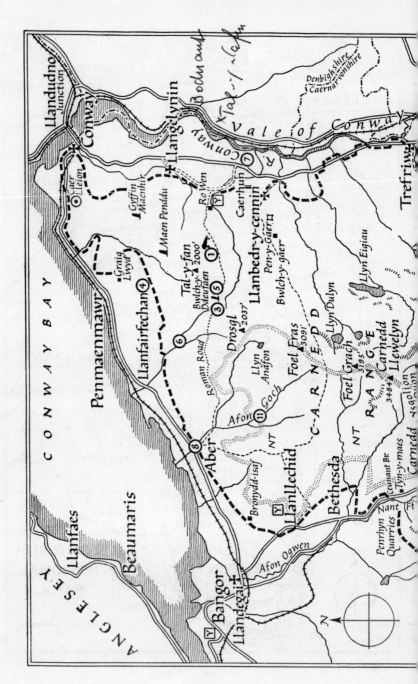

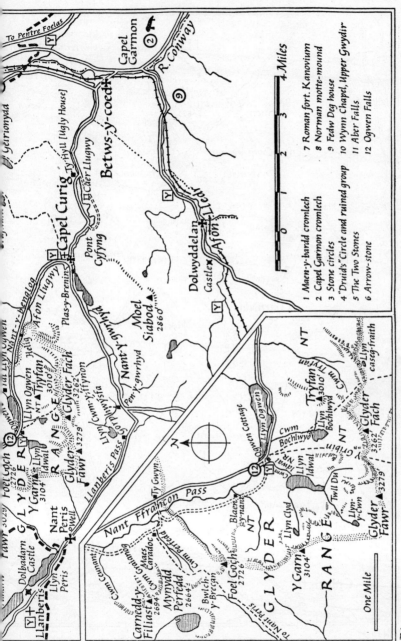

To Pentre Foelas
Capel Garmon ②
R. Conway
⑨
Betws-y-coed
Ty-Hyll [Ugly House]
Cae'r Llugwy
Capel Curig
Pont Cyfyng
Plas-y-Brenin
Afon Llugwy
Afon Llugwy
Nant-y-Benglog
Moel Siabod 2860'
Nant-y-gwryhyd
Dolwyddelan Castle
Afon Lledr
Ty'n Llyn Ogwen
Llyn Ogwen
Nant-y-benglog
Tryfan 3010'
Glyder Fach 3262'
Nant-y-gwrhyd
Cwm-y-ffynon
Cwm-y-llan
Gors-y-hwysfa

Foel Goch 3029'
Y Garn 3104'
Llyn Idwal
GLYDER RANGE
Glyder Fawr 3279'
Cwm Bochlwyd
Llyn Bochlwyd
Tryfan 3010'
Cwm Tryfan
Glyder Fach 3262'
Llyn Casegfraith
NT
NT

Dolbadarn Castle
Nant Peris
Llyn Peris
Llanberis
Llanberis Pass
Ogwen Cottage ⑫
Llyn Ogwen
Cwm Idwal
NT

Nant Ffrancon Pass
Ty Gwyn
Blaen-y-nant
Llyn Idwal
Twll Du
Llyn-y-cwn
Y Garn 3104'
Llyn Clyd
Glyder Fawr 3279'
Cribin
NT

Carnedd-y-Filiast 2694'
Gwaun-y-Gwiwnog
Cwm Graianog
Maes Caradoc
Cwm Perfedd
Mynydd Perfedd 2664'
Foel Goch 2726'
Cwm Bual
Bwlch-y-Brecan
GLYDER RANGE
To Nant Peris

N

One Mile

Map 2

1 Maen-y-bardd cromlech
2 Capel Garmon cromlech
3 Stone circles
4 "Druid's Circle and ruined group
5 The Two Stones
6 Arrow-stone
7 Roman fort, Kanovium
8 Norman motte-mound
9 Fedw Deg house
10 Wynn Chapel, Upper Gwydir
11 Aber Falls
12 Ogwen Falls

0 1 2 3 4 Miles

45

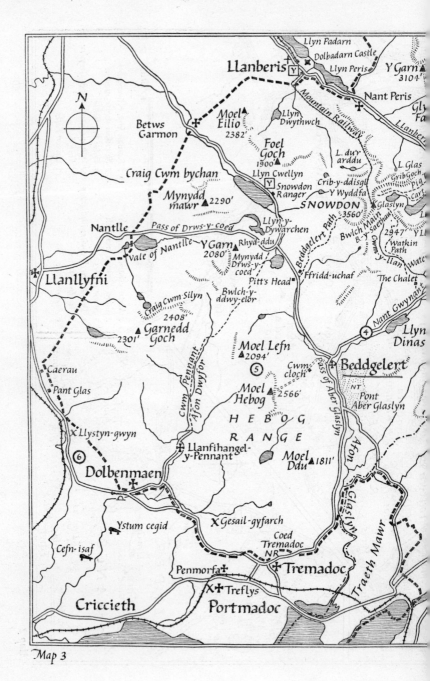

Map 3

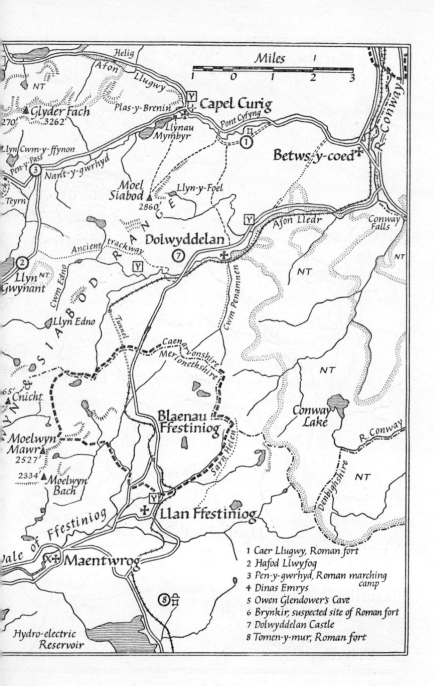

1 Caer Llugwy, Roman fort
2 Hafod Llwyfog
3 Pen-y-gwrhyd, Roman marching camp
4 Dinas Emrys
5 Owen Glendower's Cave
6 Brynkir, suspected site of Roman fort
7 Dolwyddelan Castle
8 Tomen-y-mur, Roman fort

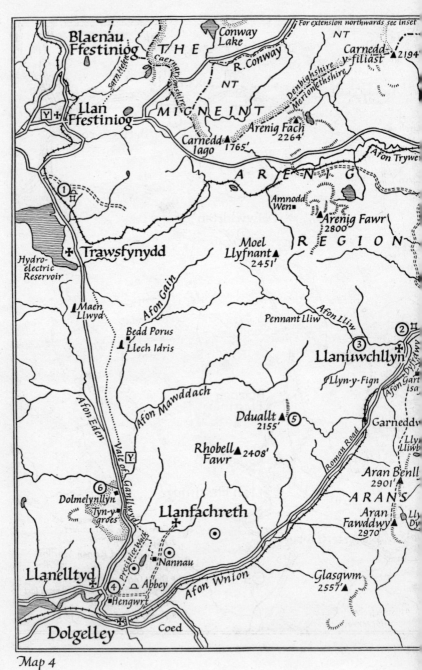

For extension northwards see inset

Blaenau Ffestiniog

Conway Lake

R. Conway

Carnedd y-filiast ▲2194'

NT

THE

Caernarvonshire

NT

Sarn-Helen

Ilan Ffestiniog

Y ✝

MIGNEINT

Denbighshire
Merionethshire

Carnedd Iago ▲1765'

Arenig Fach ▲2264'

A R E N I G

Afon Trywe

① ⌂

Amnodd Wen ■

Arenig Fawr ▲2800

Trawsfynydd ✝

Moel Llyfnant ▲2451'

R E G I O N

Hydro-electric Reservoir

Afon Gain

Pennant Lliw

Afon Lliw

② ⌂

Maen Llwyd

Bedd Porus
▲Llech Idris

Llanuwchllyn

③

✝

Afon Dyfrdwy

Llyn-y-Fign

Afon Gart isa

Afon Mawddach

Dduallt ▲ ⑤ 2155'

Garneddv

Lly Lliwb

Afon Eden

Vale of Gaullwyd

Rhobell Fawr ▲2408'

Roman Road

Aran Benll 2901'

A R A N S

⑥

Y

Dolmelynllyn

Tyn-y-groes

Llanfachreth ✝ ⊙

Aran Fawddwy ▲2970'

Lly Dy

Precipice Walk

Llanelltyd ✝

④ △ Abbey

Nannau ⊙

Afon Wnion

Glasgwm ▲2557'

Hengwrt

Dolgelley ✝

Coed

Map 4

48

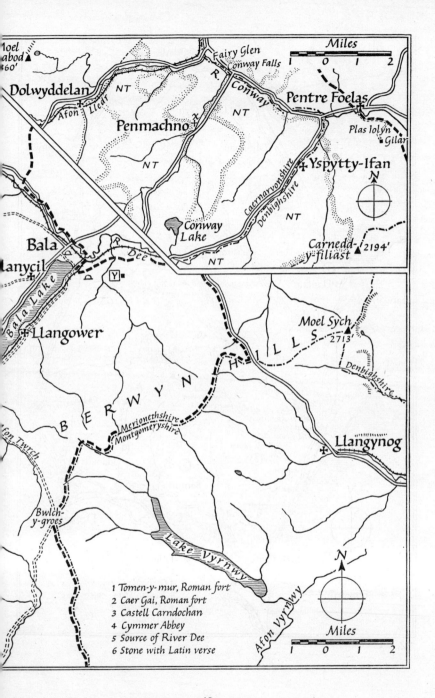

Moel
Siabod
3360'

Dolwyddelan

Afon Llcdr

NT

Penmachno

NT

NT

Fairy Glen

Conway Falls

R. Conway

NT

NT

Pentre Foelas

Plas Iolyn

Gilar

Yspytty-Ifan

Caernarvonshire

Denbighshire

NT

Conway
Lake

NT

Carnedd-
y-filiast ▲ 2194'

Miles
1   0   1   2

N

Bala

Llanycil

Dee

Y

Bala Lake

Llangower

BERWYN   HILLS

Moel Sych
2713'

Denbighshire

Merionethshire
Montgomeryshire

Llangynog

Afon Twrch

Bwlch-
y-groes

Lake Vyrnwy

Afon Vyrnwy

1 Tomen-y-mur, Roman fort
2 Caer Gai, Roman fort
3 Castell Carndochan
4 Cymmer Abbey
5 Source of River Dee
6 Stone with Latin verse

N

Miles
1   0   1   2

49

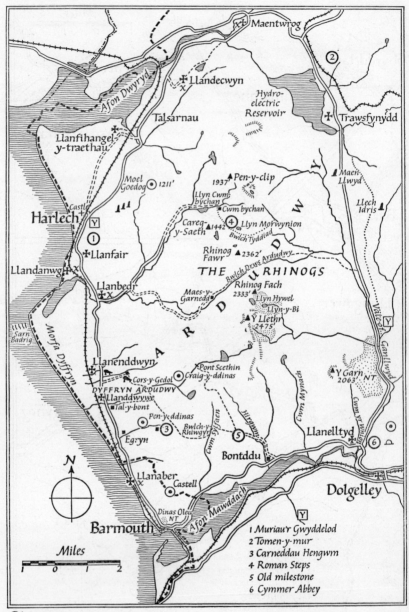

Maentwrog

②

Llandecwyn

Hydro-
electric
Reservoir

Talsarnau

Trawsfynydd

Llanfihangel-
y-traethau

Maen
Llwyd

Moel
Goedog 1211'

Llech
Idris

Pen-y-clip
1937

Castle

Llyn Cwm
bychan

Harlech

Y

Cwm bychan

①

Llanfair

Careg-
y-Saeth 1442

④ Llyn Morwynion

Bwlch Tyddiad

Llandanwg X

Rhinog
Fawr 2362'

THE RHINOGS

Bwlch Drws Ardudwy

Llanbedr
X

Maes-y-
Garnedd

Rhinog Fach
2333'

A R D U D W Y

Llyn Hywel

Llyn-y-Bi

Sarn
Badrig

Morfa Dyffryn

Y Llethr
2475'

Llanenddwyn

Pont Scethin
Craig-y-ddinas

Y Garn
2063 NT

Cors-y-Gedol

DYFFRYN ARDUDWY

Llanddwywe

Cwm Mynach

Vale of Gamllwyd

Tal-y-bont

Pen-y-ddinas

Y

③

Bwlch-y-
Rhiwgyr

⑤

Cwm yr wnin

Egryn

Llanelltyd

⑥

N

Bontddu

Llanaber
X

Castell

Dolgelley

Dinas Oleu
NT

Afon Mawddach

Y

Barmouth

Miles

1   0   1   2

1 Muriau'r Gwyddelod
2 Tomen-y-mur
3 Carneddau Hengwm
4 Roman Steps
5 Old milestone
6 Cymmer Abbey

Map 5

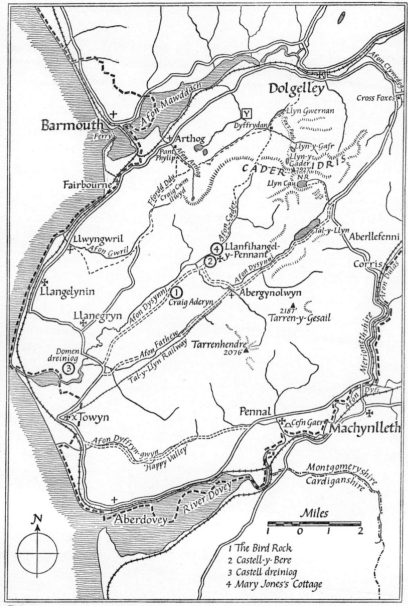

Miles

1 0 1 2

1 The Bird Rock
2 Castell-y-Bere
3 Castell dreiniog
4 Mary Jones's Cottage

Map 6

51

7

The People and the Language

IN attempting to describe 850 square miles of extremely varied country which is packed full of interest, scenic, archaeological, historical, and human, in a comparatively few pages, what method should one adopt? If it is essential to give as nearly as possible *all* the facts the form must be that of an inventory—the dry bones. This would be well enough for reference but not for reading. If the Guide is to serve as an introduction to parts of the Park unknown to the reader, so that he can judge before setting out whether it is the sort of country he wants to see, or contains the things likely to interest him, then it must be readable and descriptive. That is the treatment I have tried to give, using what is almost a narrative form to conduct him from point to point over each of the several mountain ranges in turn, sometimes pointing out objects *en route*, at other times summing them up under category heads. In this process information occasionally gets scattered instead of concentrated. Cross-references and the Index will, I hope, prove some remedy.

The mountains fall naturally into two main groups—the five ranges in Caernarvonshire (with a small part of Denbighshire included) covered by the old Welsh name *Eryri* equated by the Italianate-English *Snowdonia*, and the three ranges in the south which lie within the County of Merioneth. Lacking an over-all name authorized by tradition I have included them under the old Welsh derivative of the name of that shire—*Meirion*.

The points I have tried to make are these. To show what are the individual scenic characteristics of each mountain range. To describe ways up and across the mountains (the Reader being presumed an average walker but not a mountaineer). To indicate the location of prehistoric remains, early Christian memorials, and parish churches within the Park boundary or lying just outside. All these things are intimately bound up with the folk who live in the hills and valleys— descendants of the 'Ancient British' of the history book, the 'Iron Age Celts' of archaeology, who lived in 'hut-circles' and constructed the great earthwork 'hill-forts'. Furthermore, in this mountain country, an infusion of blood from earlier races must still be circulating and it is not impossible that certain old grey stones on a man's sheepwalk may cover the dust of an ancestor who lived as much as four thousand years ago.

The early Christian memorials (Plate V), those rough pillar-stones bearing simple epitaphs in Latin which are mainly of the fifth–sixth century (within living memory of the Roman Occupation), mark the graves of members of the native Church which was established in Britain at least 300 years before the missionary, Augustine, landed in Kent to convert the heathen Saxons and build the first cathedral at Canterbury. Most of the parish churches in Wales were founded in that early period of Celtic Christianity, though their visible fabric could in no case be traced to an earlier date than the twelfth century. Their story is therefore quite different from that of the parish churches of England. Their interest is of a different kind and deserves separate attention and study. In the following there is no room to give them more than a passing mention. They reflect the simplicity and homeliness of their worshippers, the Welsh hillmen, down fourteen centuries of time, rather than architectural graces.

To English visitors I would like to say something on the subject of Welsh place-names about which they seem to be in constant difficulties. They are beautiful things, apt, interpretive of local situations, and they often preserve facts and names of historical interest.

To give these words their due they should be pronounced in a way that is a near approximation to their sound-values. By this I don't mean a perfect mimicry of certain sounds that are quite foreign to the English mouth but a good working compromise. Through a curious failure of the education system of the United Kingdom children in English schools are not warned that while the sister nation uses the same alphabet, all the letters have not the same sound-values as those to which they are accustomed. Through the lack of this elementary key English visitors innocently apply the phonetics they have learned, usually with hideously cacophonous results. Yet the number of letters with altered sounds is very small, amounting only to six single and three double ones. The singles are i, e, u, y, w, and f; the doubles are ll, dd, and ch.

To begin with the doubles, the ll is, and always has been, a settler to the Anglo-Saxon. The name Floyd represents one of his early attempts to say Lloyd. The compromise of pronouncing it as if the double l were single has been much more successful and can be recommended for use with Welsh names in English talk where the ll comes first, and as '*th*' where it comes later in the word. By this convention the Anglicised version of Llangollen would be *Langothlen*.

The dd is quite straightforward. It is simply a thick *th* as in 'thee and thou'. There is nothing foreign in sound to the English tongue about this, as the Saxons used a crossed d (ð) for exactly the same thing, as Scandinavian countries still do. The great thing to remember is that the double d is *always* a thick th. Where the thin sound is intended, as in the English words 'hath' and 'thanks', th is used, and in Welsh, th is *always* the thin sound.

The ch is just an ordinary guttural which the English also used in Chaucer's time and their German cousins still do. People who tell Irish stories with much 'Och sure!' in the dialogue find no difficulty with it.

As to the single letters, the u and y have a subtle inflection in the Welsh that is harder for the Englishman to learn than the proper way to say ll. But the plain equivalent of English i for Welsh u is near enough to render the sound of place-names euphonious instead of ugly. Thus Llandudno should be *Landidno*. But this i sound is, as it were, a near-miss for an e, and more of an e than an i at the end of a word. Thus du (black) is nearly imitated by *dee*, though, as I said, in the mouth of a Welshman this inflection is exceedingly subtle and although *dee* is well enough for a rough-and-ready rendering of du, the sound is not quite that of the English double e. This duty is done by i. Min (edge) is *meen*, ci (dog) is *kee*, a reminder that the c is always hard, s being used for the soft sound.

Letter e can have the usual short sound, as in pen (head or upper part) which is pronounced the same in both languages but, like the French e, it is more commonly sounded as the a in day; hen (old) is *haine*, te (tea) is *tay*.

This takes us to the y. The name of the letter is 'er' and when found singly (meaning 'the' or 'of the') it is pronounced *er*. Thus the mountain Y Garn (The Heap) is *Er Garn*. But it has two other values. In the early part of a word it is a u, in the latter part an i. The river Ystwyth is *Ustwith*, and Abergynolwyn, *Abergunolwin*. Cynon (where it occurs singly but nearer the beginning) is *Cunon*. Gwyn (where it is nearer the end) is *Gwin*.

The w has the sound of oo and only varies between a long and short stress as happens in English also between such words as book (short) and loot (long). Cwm, *Coom* (a valley blocked at the upper end or a mountain hollow) and Bwlch, *Boolch* (a mountain pass) have the short oo sound, while cwn, *coon* (dogs), bedw, *bedoo* (birch) are sounded long, which is usual for most words.

Although v is used in Welsh mediaeval inscriptions on tombs this letter has become extinct in the Welsh alphabet and f is used instead and given the full sound value of v. Felin Hen (Old Mill) is *Vellin Haine*. The double f I have not bracketed with the double letters as it is no different from the same in English—in puff, for example. Where its use differs in modern Welsh is that it is the sole representative of the f sound, the single f, as just stated, being in all cases pronounced as v.

Set out briefly and roughly, then, the values are:

Welsh	English
ll	No exact equivalent. A convention suggested.
dd	Thick th
ch	As in the Caledonian 'It's a braw nicht, the nicht.'
i	Long e (as English ee)
e	a (as in day)
u	i (as in did)
y	u (as in bun) or when standing alone as er
w	oo
f	v

In Welsh, as in Latin, the adjective comes after, and not before, the noun; thus 'White House' is 'Ty (House) Gwyn (White)'.

When the unfamiliar change of sound values in letters of the alphabet has been overcome it will be found that Welsh is a strictly phonetic language—which is far from being the case of English. But there remains one more difficulty. It lies in the changes of spelling which take place when words stand in particular relationship to each other, and is called *mutation*. It is done chiefly to make the flow of speech more euphonious, an amenity of which the native poets have taken full advantage. It will be sufficient for the present purpose to name five cases where the first letter of a word is likely to be affected and changed for another under which it cannot be looked up in the dictionary. The most common alterations are these:

Words beginning (in the dictionary) with	P	B	M	C	T
may change those initial letters to	B	F	F	G	D

So that *pont* would become *bont*, *bryn* would be *fryn*, *moel* would be *foel*, *carn* would be *garn*, and *tref* be *dref*.

Welsh place-names and topographical features are very much easier to derive, and therefore to understand, than those in England. Most of them are in plain language and only need to be translated to find the meaning. They are nearly all descriptive and mostly compounded of the elements in the following list.

Some common components of Welsh names likely to be found in all parts of the Park, with suffixes which, when added, form the plural are—

Mountains
1 Small hill *Bryn -iau*
2 Bare-topped hill *Moel -ydd*
3 Mountain *Mynydd -oedd*
4 Summit or head *Pen -nau*
5 Extremity (often head of a valley) *Blaen -au*
6 Head of a valley (usually one blocked by a mountain cirque) *Cwm-Cymoedd*

7   Steep place *Rhiw -iau*
8   Valley *Nant* pl. *Nentydd*, or *Dyffryn -noedd*
9   Pass *Bwlch* pl. *Bylchau*

By poetic analogy

10 Back *Cefn -au*
11 Breast *Bron -nydd*
12 Cheek *Boch -au*
13 Door *Drws* pl. *Drysau* (used for narrow mountain pass)
14 Ladder *Ysgol -ion*
15 Table *Bwrdd* pl. *Byrddau*
16 Chair *Cadair* or *Cader* pl. *Cadeiriau*
17 Comb *Crib -au*
18 Hay-rake *Cribin -iau*
19 Water *Dwfr* or *Dwr*
20 River *Afon -ydd*
21 Waterfall *Pistyll -oedd*
22 Bog *Cors -ydd*
23 Wet ground *Gwern -i* (*see* 41)
24 Ford *Rhyd -ydd*
25 Stepping-stones or causeway *Sarn -au*
26 Bridge *Pont -ydd*
27 Road *Ffordd* pl. *Ffyrdd*
28 Lane *Lon -ydd*
29 House *Ty* pl. *Tai*
30 Mill *Melin -au*
31 Stone *Maen* pl. *Meini*
32 Stone slab *Llech -au*
33 Rock *Carreg* pl. *Cerrig*
34 Cave *Ogof* or *Ogo* pl. *Ogofau*
35 Field *Maes* pl. *Meysydd*, or *Cae -au*, or *Dol* pl. *Dolydd*
36 Patch of cultivation wrested from the open mountain *Fridd -oedd*
37 A Tree *Coeden* pl. *Coed*
38 A Wood *Coed -ydd*

Tree and Plant Names

39 Oak *Derwen* pl. *Derw*
40 Ash *Onnen* pl. *Onn* or *Ynn*
41 Alder *Gwernen -ni* (Compare with No. 23)
42 Birch *Bedwen* pl. *Bedw*
43 Holly *Celynen* pl. *Celyn*
44 Gorse *Eithinen* pl. *Eithin*
45 Heather *Grug*

Adjectives

46 Big *Mawr*
47 Little *Bach* or (masc.) *Bychan* (fem.) *Bechan*

48   Long *Hir*
49   Uppermost *Uchaf*
50   Middle *Canol*
51   Lowest *Isaf*
52   Old *Hen*
53   New *Newydd*
54   Black *Du*
55   White *Gwyn* (fem.) *Gwen*
56   Grey or Brown *Llwyd*
57   Blue or Green *Glas*
58   Red *Coch*

In descriptive names the definite article often acts as genitive and stands for 'of the'; thus *Pen-y-bryn* is Top-of-the-Hill and *Pont-y-Gwr-Drwg* is Bridge-of-the-Naughty-Man or The Devil's Bridge.

To make quick direct reference from Welsh names in the Guide or on the map to the above list this alphabetical index is provided, each word being numbered as in the list.

Afon 20, Bach 47, Bechan 47, Bedw 42, Blaen 5, Boch 12, Bron 11, Byrddau 15, Bryn 1, Bwlch 9, Bychan 47, Bylchau 9, Bwrdd 15, Cadair 16, Cader 16, Canol 50, Carreg 33, Cae 35, Cefn 10, Celyn 43, Cerrig 33, Coch 58, Coed 38, Cors 22, Crib 17, Cribin 18, Cwm 6, Derwen 39, Dol 35, Drws 13, Drysau 13, Du 54, Dwfr 19, Dwr 19, Dyffryn 8, Eithin 44, Ffordd 27, Ffridd 36, Glas 57, Grug 45, Gwen 55, Gwern 23, Gwernen 41, Gwyn 55, Hen 52, Hir 48, Isaf 51, Llech 32, Lon 28, Llwyd 56, Maen 31, Maes 35, Mawr 46, Meini 31, Meysydd 35, Moel 2, Mynydd 3, Nant 8, Nentydd 8, Newydd 53, Ogo 34, Onnen 40, Pen 4, Pistyll 21, Pont 26, Rhiw 7, Sarn 25, Tai 29, Uchaf 49, Ynn 40, Ysgol 14.

The above is arranged according to the English order of letters and not the Welsh, whose alphabet ends 'u w y', pronounced *ee oo er*. This triplet is rather like the expression universal in all languages used by bathers entering the sea early in the year—a useful tag to memory for sound differences of those letters.

There is a human figure without whom the National Park would lose so much of its charm and character that we might, with due respect, describe him as one of the chief amenities. This is the hill farmer. He and his forebears have lived lives so hard in toil and exposure as might have been expected to blunt the finer senses. Yet nearly always it is with these that he is endowed above the average. He is a keen observer of nature, with a genius for collecting local lore and a unique gift for imparting it with dramatic force, salted with real wit. And nearly always he is wonderfully courteous and helpful to strangers. And strangers may share, at least by watching the great spectacular events in the hill-farmers' year—bringing down the sheep from the mountain in the early summer to wash and clip, the dogs scouring the mountain side and marshalling them by companies into the great many-roomed pen built in cyclopean dry-stone, like a prehistoric fortress, beside the river and the washing-pool. A week later, down at the farm, the shearing takes place. Hand-clippers are still in general use and often there is a speed contest among the older hands. There is another gathering of the flocks in August, when they are brought down for antiseptic dipping. Next come the sheep sales held at some farm centrally placed—a more picturesque foregathering of men and dogs than those at the town 'marts'. Then there are the sheep-dog trials. The local ones are usually held in the late Autumn after the sheep sales though the larger events may be held earlier. They are generally well advertised in advance and always worth seeing.

In the old days the hill farmer and his family spent the year in two different abodes. In the winter months they lived in the more substantial house and buildings—the *hendre*—in the valley bottom. Early in the year, after the spring sowing in the arable land, they migrated with their animals (chiefly cows and goats) to the smaller house—*hafod*—on the summer pasture high up in the hills. In the Llanberis valley a relic of this time-honoured practice still goes on, the cattle being taken up to summer pasture where they are duly milked in the evening but there is no longer a family migration. Elsewhere, the custom has long been given up. But the old hafods can still be seen scattered in places so remote and high up in the hills that a stranger may well wonder who on earth could have lived there.

The ruins of these buildings have hardly yet attracted the attention of the antiquary or become dignified by the name of 'ancient monument'. But they lie in pleasant solitudes, usually where a spring of sweet water bubbles out among fragrant herbage and where the mountain air is good and strong. Seldom is there more to be seen than bare foundations composed of immense stones with traces of paddock walls adjoining. Yet they strike the imagination vividly by the very silence they preserve about the folk who came up to spend the long summer days there, year after year and generation after generation.

8

Snowdonia

NOTES ON THE FOLLOWING TEXT

THE abbreviation M. is used to indicate a reference to the one-inch Ordnance map, Seventh Series Edition (1953). Distances for cross-country routes are taken from the map with a little more allowance for ups and downs than the cartographer's 'horizontal equivalent' but, as they are not measured on the ground, they are bound to be rough and a little optimistic. The expression *mountain gate* means the gate through the last wall of the enclosed lower lands on to the open mountain.

In spite of what I have said about Welsh being a purely phonetic language there is some discrepancy in the spelling of place-names. There is an old established traditional spelling and recently there has been introduced an amended orthography based on recommendations of the Board of Celtic Studies. These are not in universal use. Some have been adopted in official quarters but here, too, there is discrepancy. A case in point is the spelling of Bettws-y-Coed. It has been thus written for a very long while. But the Celtic scholars say that a double t is a superfluity in a Welsh word and that one t should be struck out. The Post Office and the Railway now spell the name with only one t. This form is followed in the latest edition of the half-inch Bartholomew map[1] (an unofficial publication) whereas the latest Ordnance map (named above) sticks to the double t. There are several other divergences between these two maps which are both in general use by people on holiday. In my own renderings I have tried to make as fair an adjustment as possible, while deferring to my contributors (two of them 'good Welshmen') and mainly following their preferences.

The Carnedd Range

The name is chosen for convenience from the two highest mountains in the group, *Carnedd Llewelyn* (3,484 feet, next highest to Snowdon) and *Carnedd Dafydd* (3,426 feet). They are of particular interest among the mountains with personal names as they are quite obviously called after the last native Prince of Wales and his brother. Other

---

[1] Sheets 22 and 27 for the Park.

summits over 3,000 feet are *Foel Grach* (3,195 feet) and *Foel Fras* (3,091 feet). All these hill-tops lie roughly in a line north-and-south with long intervals of high ground in between them. They form the backbone of the range. It is about five miles from Carnedd Dafydd to Foel Fras—all on the skyline, with long views on either hand.

Most of the *lakes* in the group have been appropriated for reservoirs of power or supply. *Cowlyd* is the largest. It supplies Colwyn Bay with water and is linked by an open leet with *Llugwy* and by tunnel with *Eigiau*. It holds some of the largest trout though they are hardly to be lured except by live bait. Over it stands a mountain with such a sharply cut profile that it can be picked out at once from as far off as Llandudno Junction. It is called appropriately *Pen Llithrig-y-Wrach*—the Witch's Slide. *Dulyn* (the Black Lake) lies under towering and impressive crags. It sends water to Llandudno, and *Llyn Anafon* (lovely, and quite untamed until lately) now sends water to Llanfairfechan. *Crafnant* is one of the most charming and little altered from its natural self, though the scrub oak woodland that once enhanced it has been replaced by coniferous plantations. *Ffynnon Lloer* is still a wild lake, untouched and unspoilt.

CROSS-COUNTRY

Along the length of the range from Nant Ffrancon to Llanfairfechan. You must first get up Carnedd Dafydd. The ascent from Tal Llyn Ogwen Farm, at the upper end of Ogwen Lake, is steep but quite easy. By following the stream up you come to the hollow wherein lies Ffynon Lloer and from thence you may pick your way to the top. Between Carnedd Dafydd and Carnedd Llewelyn you will walk above the edge of the great precipice of Ysgolion Duon—the Black Ladders, one of the outstanding scenic features of the group, and then keep the high ground all the way to Foel Fras. From there you can see Llyn Anafon (or Aber Lake) lying below in the northern hollow and find your way down to it or the lower Anafon Valley where there is a clear track to Llanfairfechan. The walk is about 13 miles.

Across the range. There is a footpath across the broadest part of the range indicated on M. It follows an old pack-horse track from Bwlch-y-Gaer Farm, Llanbedr-y-cennin, to Bronnyddisaf Farm at the far corner of the range, with branches to Aber and Llanllechid. This passes the interesting Celtic fort of *Pen-y-Gaer* (page 25) and crosses the high ridge just south of Foel Fras. The walk is about 11 miles.

The Roman road from Caerhun (Conovium) to Caernarvon (Segontium) is followed from either Llanbedr-y-cennin or Ro Wen. At the gate to the open mountain it becomes a green track which is well marked all the way to Aber. It crosses the range at the Gap of

Two Stones (Bwlch-y-Ddeufaen) between Drosgl (2,036 feet) and Tal-y-Fan (2,000 feet). The *Two Stones* are prehistoric monoliths of indeterminable date. There is a *stone circle* in a field near the mountain gate on the south side of the track (not very conspicuous) and the *cromlech* called Maen-y-bardd (The bard's Stone) (Plate IVb) a little way from the mountain gate on the Ro Wen side. Three Roman milestones have been discovered on this part of the road.

The green track ends at a gate into the lane leading down to Aber village, about a mile-and-a-half away, where it joins the coast road. By the bridge where the lane crosses the Anafon River a footpath leads to the *waterfalls* of the tributary, Afon Goch. The lower fall, a 60 foot drop, is an old tourist favourite. Near the junction of the lane and main road is a green mound, a relic of the *motte-and-bailey castle* of Llewelyn the Great whose wife was Joan, natural daughter of King John.[1] The distance from Ro Wen to Aber is about nine miles.

Between Capel Curig and Trefriw. From Capel Curig a footpath leads over the open moorland to the head of the deep cwm in which lies *Crafnant Lake,* giving a fine view overlooking it before descending to its shore. From the Lake there is a road down to Trefriw. A footpath links Crafnant and its rather plainer sister, *Geirionydd* (about a mile to the east). Half way between Betws-y-Coed and Capel Curig, by Ty Hyll (Ugly House) and the main road bridge over the Llugwy, is a rough road which leads direct to Lake Geirionydd and thence to Trefriw (its church noted below). By making a slight deviation on the way down one comes to the still older and more interesting parish church of *Llanrychwyn* (Plate Vc). From here a footpath leads to Llanrwst.

SURROUNDINGS

The eastern side of the range is bounded by the *Conway Valley* from which it rises with a steep almost cliff-like front making the formidable military barrier which for so long preserved the independence of Upper Gwynedd. Its boundary rested on this line, as also does that of the National Park. The *Roman road* from Carmarthen (called *Sarn Helen*) comes down the valley to Caerhun, where it joined the road from Chester to Caernarvon at the fort of *Conovium*[2] whose ramparts are still plain to be seen.

---

[1] From Aber there was an ancient route across the sands at low tide to Anglesey, still in regular use until the nineteenth century. Before the founding of Beaumaris by the English in 1295 this route would have led to the Franciscan Friary at Llanfaes, and here Princess Joan, who died in 1237, was taken for burial. Her stone coffin and effigy is now in the parish church at Beaumaris.

[2] So spelt on M. though it is KANOVIUM on the milestone (now in the British Museum).

The south-west is skirted, from Betws-y-Coed to Bangor by Telford's Holyhead Road (A.5) which follows the Llugwy Valley through Capel Curig up into Nant-y-Benglog, then through the Pass of Nant Ffrancon and down that valley (watered by the River Ogwen) to the sea. About half way between Betws-y-Coed and Capel Curig is another Roman fort whose presence (though suspected earlier) was only proved in 1920 when excavations were undertaken. As its Roman name could not be traced it was given a new one and called Caer Llugwy.[1] It lies between the main road bridge and the next one up-stream, Pont Cyfyng, on the right bank of the river, by the side-road connecting the two bridges, which is a portion of the turnpike way made in 1805 before Telford's road was constructed. The earthwork ramparts are fairly well marked. Most of the finds of the 1920-22 excavation are in the Museum of Welsh Archaeology in Bangor.

On the northern front of the range, overlooking the sea, the Park boundary lies mainly along the higher ground and only descends to touch the coast road for a short distance at Aber. At Penmaenmawr, it runs nearly two miles inland and the well-known *Druid's Circle* (now ascribed to the Bronze Age) is just outside it. On these wide open moors a great many prehistoric remains lie scattered, among them the enigmatic *arrow-stones*. These are boulders marked by grooves which look exactly like those so often seen outside old churches and other mediaeval buildings. They are clearly the result of sharpening implements of some kind, though exactly what sort has never been decided. But prehistoric examples are very rare and, in Wales, seem to be confined to the northern fringe of this range. A fair guess would be that they were associated with the large industry of weapon production from the local igneous rock at Graig Lwyd (Penmaenmawr) established in late Neolithic times.[2] The finest of these arrow-stones is on a boulder-strewn bit of waste ground a quarter of a mile south of Cammarnaint Farm, above Llanfairfechan—a large flat rock, eight feet long with more than a hundred cuts on the top. It is just within the Park boundary.

The following *old churches*, within or just outside the Park are interesting. *Conway* and *Llanrwst* have fine rood-screens—the latter, complete with loft. At Llanrwst, the Wynns of Gwydir Castle built two private chapels, one attached to the parish church (1633), another at Upper Gwydir (1673). The latter is intact with its contemporary

[1] So marked on M., but not on the Ordnance Map of Roman Britain, where it is called after the farm, Bryn-y-Gefeiliau.

[2] The best account of the arrow-stones is in 'The Heart of Northern Wales' by W. Bezant Lowe. For Graig Lwyd industry, 'Caernarvonshire' Vol. I, Royal Commission on Ancient Monuments.

furniture. Llanrychwyn (700 feet) has already been mentioned; *Llangelynin*, at the north-east corner of the Park is still higher up (900 feet) and more out-of-the-way. Both are sixth century foundations, a time when, no doubt, the uplands were still populated. *Caerhun* church is placed within the (then) protected area of the Roman fort of Conovium. *Llanbedr-y-cennin* has the same charm of simplicity as the foregoing and so has the older church at *Capel Curig*. *Trefriw* has an excellent mediaeval roof and a remarkable pulpit. *Llandegai* contains the tomb of Archbishop Williams and his monument with the helmet he is believed to have worn at the siege of Conway (1645).

Knights who fought under the Black Prince in the French wars of Edward III have effigies at Llanrwst and *Betws-y-Coed*. The effigy at Betws-y-Coed has interesting links with past and present. It represents Grufyd ap Davyd Goch[1] (a grandson of the unfortunate Prince David, the brother of Llewelyn the last native Prince of Wales). This knight lived at *Fedw Deg* (pron. Vedoo Dayg) on the hill above the junction of the rivers Lledr and Conway. The ruin of a sixteenth century house, standing on the older foundation and adjoining the farm of the same name shown on our map, has recently been put into a state of preservation and its woodwork renovated by the Ministry of Works. On the hillside, below the present road to the farm are the remains of the ancient approach by *horse-steps*, similar to the Roman Steps at Cwm Bychan (page 86), traceable in places though much decayed. This is still known locally as *Llwybr Gruffydd ap Dafydd Goch* (The Path of Griffith, son of Red David).

The Denbighshire Portion of the Park

This is shaped roughly like the segment of an orange, the curved part being the right bank of the Conway from Pentre Foelas to a point between Betws-y-Coed and Llanrwst where the river makes a turn from the middle flat ground towards the escarpment on the western side of the Valley and passes under the railway line. At this bridge the boundary of the Park strikes eastward till it touches the old coach road from Llanrwst to Pentre Foelas, following that road (the straight side of the segment) to the latter place.

All that part lies in Denbighshire, on the fringe of the Hiraethog Hills, a wide range extending between the Conway Valley and the Vale of Clwyd, its higher ground a wild open region of grass-moors and lakes.

[1] Contemporary spelling (fourteenth century) as on tomb.

But this countryside within the Park has long since been tamed or partly tamed. With its numerous small hills and streams (and a farm in every hollow), it is laced with lanes, tracks, and footpaths and delightful to explore on foot, a strong sense of the half-wild still clinging to its scenery.

In the middle of the district is the principal village, Capel Garmon, near which is the *Capel Garmon Cromlech* (Plate IV a), the remains of a long barrow which was put into a state of preservation by the Office of Works in 1924. It consists of three burial chambers approached by a passage from a point midway along the side of the (former) mound. The original mound which covered the barrow was surrounded by a stone curb which was cleared during the excavation and is now plainly seen on the turf. It shows the indented or 'horned' feature at the broader end, thought to be either a false entrance or ritual shrine. Only the western chamber retains its covering capstone. An earlier explorer of the tomb found this chamber converted into a stable with a wooden door and stone manger. The long mound had been composed of loose stones and not earth, and the antiquary, Edward Lhwyd, visiting it in 1699 compared it with the long cairns of Hen Gwm (page 84) which still retain much of their covering. A further note on the Denbighshire portion is on page 88.

The Glyder Range

As seen on the map, this range looks not unlike a Christmas stocking, with the Pass of Nant Ffrancon at the instep, the Pass of Llanberis at the back of the heel, and the wider valley of Nant-y-Gwryd at the sole. It is formed by a continuous ridge which rises in altitude from the Bethesda slate quarries in the north to a level platform occupied by a small shallow lake called *Llyn-y-Cwn*—the Lake of the Dogs. This is rather like the landing on a staircase, giving pause and forming a turning-point. Beyond it the ground rises abruptly towards the highest point, *Glyder Fawr* (3,279 feet) just a thousand feet above the lake, and at the same time the ridge turns through almost a right angle towards the east. This point is what I have called the 'instep' and, scenically, it may be called the most eventful corner in North Wales.

The stream flowing out of this little lake falls into the extraordinary chasm called Twll Du—the Black Hole—more widely known as the *Devil's Kitchen*. The most striking vision of the cleft is to be had from the point where the stream is engulfed. From here one looks down through the gap to *Idwal Lake* (again) just a thousand feet below.

The whole ridge facing this way, that is, overlooking Nant Ffrancon and Nant-y-Benglog is scalloped with hollows gouged out during the Ice Age with their lower lips well above the valley bottom and therefore called by geologists Hanging valleys. The rock bastions dividing them are surmounted by moderate peaks, rather in the manner of flying-buttresses topped by pinnacles. This makes one of the distinctive features of Nant Ffrancon Pass.

So much is the Ice Age in Britain now taken for granted that it is hard to believe that little more than a century ago such a condition was not even suspected by the leading geologists. Darwin, recalling his visit to Nant Ffrancon with Professor Adam Sedgwick in 1831, wrote 'We spent many hours in Cwm Idwal, examining all the rocks with extreme care, as Sedgwick was anxious to find fossils in them; but neither of us saw a trace of the wonderful glacial phenomena all around us; we did not notice the plainly scored rocks, the perched boulders, the lateral and terminal moraines. Yet these phenomena are so conspicuous that, as I declared in a paper published many years afterwards in the *Philosophical Magazine*, a house burnt down by fire did not tell its story more plainly than did this valley.' But Sedgwick refused to believe in the glacial theory till the end of his days—which were not numbered until 1873.

Cwm Idwal (Plate IX) remains one of the most perfect testaments to that remote prehistoric time before human records began to be made. Not only are all those evidences noted by Darwin preserved with quite incredible freshness but there is actually a living link in the shape of a rare alpine flora which followed the retreating ice up into its last high strongholds and has never died out. This great natural museum is now protected as a Nature Reserve and under the care of an officially appointed warden. It is not only the plant-robber who menaces conservation here but also the less-suspected rock-climber who in times past has scarified rock surfaces indiscriminately and denuded whole ledges of their moss and mountain turf canopies. This is worse than tearing pages out of a book, for replenishment may take long ages and the same story will never be repeated.

In the Museum of Geology at South Kensington there is a model showing an attempted restoration of Nant Ffrancon as it appeared in the Ice Age. The main glacier is seen to be issuing from Cwm Idwal and grinding down Nant Ffrancon above which those 'hanging valleys' are each generating a glacier of their own. The most perfect specimen of the latter is Cwm Graianog. Its floor has been deeply cleft by its glacier, but this gash has been filled by a debris of loose stones on the retreat of the ice, so that the valley has now a saucer-like floor with a moraine forming a neat semicircular rim as regular as a prehistoric earthwork.

But the stream which rises there follows the old rock channel under the loose stones and gushes out far below the lip of the moraine. The comely shape of this moraine has earned it the name (in Welsh) of the Maiden's Arm.

The whole range can be traversed from end to end without difficulty. It takes the best part of a day and if you hug the skyline by skirting the edge of all the cwms and topping all the eminences it can hardly be less than 15 miles. The Penrhyn slate quarries occupy the extreme northern tip of the ridge which one must outflank either to the west or east. The latter gives the easiest access. You leave the main road at the lower end of Nant Ffrancon and cross the Ogwen at Ceunant Bridge. Following this old road (called Roman, but actually constructed in the latter part of the eighteenth century to facilitate the passage to Westminster of Irish M.Ps.) to the gate at the fenced portion, a stile, immediately to the right of the gate, puts you down on the open mountain. From here, by keeping well to the right of the stream, you reach the crest of the ridge overlooking Cwm Ceunant, the first of the series of hollows. *Cwm Graianog* is the next one. Its northern buttress is dominated by *Carnedd-y-Filiast* (2,694 feet) and looking down into the hollow there is another interesting thing to be seen besides the remains of glaciation—and far more ancient. The large smooth slabs of rock forming the buttress are slightly corrugated with gentle undulations. They are fragments of an ancient sea beach where tides ebbed and flowed in that very remote geological time now labelled Upper Cambrian, preserved intact as a huge fossil with ripple-marks on the sand, worm-casts, and the fern-like trails of marine creatures. Beside this relic of a vanished horizon (now tilted at an angle of 45 degrees) the Ice Age seems a very recent event.

Carnedd-y-Filiast (The Cairn of the Greyhound-bitch) is quickly succeeded by *Mynydd Perfedd* (2,665 feet). Just here there is a cwm on either side of the ridge, which only happens once again—between the Glyders. That on the west contains the shapely lake called Marchlyn (Lake of the Stallion), beyond which stands the peak, *Elidir Fawr* (3,030 feet). This mountain has a very striking profile, like that of the Matterhorn, when seen from the upper slopes of Carnedd Dafydd. At that distance it looks tremendous but the summit is quite easy to reach from Mynydd Perfedd.

In contrast to the escarpment over Nant Ffrancon, a long grassy slope leads down on the reverse side to Nant Peris, beyond which Snowdon stands up majestically and there is a clear view to its summit. The next high point along the ridge is *Foel Goch* (2,727 feet), a fine pyramidal shape as seen from the valley below. Between Mynydd Perfedd and it there is a gentle dip in the skyline called *Bwlch-y-Brecan*.

The remains of a pack-horse track shows that this pass was once regularly used as a route between the two valleys. Foel Goch is succeeded by *Y Garn* (3,104 feet) with little *Llyn Clyd* in the hollow below, a lake full of small hungry trout. Then you come to that platform I have called a 'landing' at the instep of the range. Only a little way beyond the great rift of the Devil's Kitchen (up which only the expert climber can venture) there is a cairn marking the beginning of a direct and quite easy way down into Cwm Idwal.

There is only a difference of seventeen feet between the *Glyders*, Great and Little (3,279 and 3,262 feet, respectively), and the latter is the more prominent and cuts the more important figure, seen from below. These blunt excrescences composed of rucks of loose weathered grey slabs which send forth moaning sounds in certain winds are quite the wildest and weirdest of the Welsh summits (Plate X a). There is a direct way up from the lower end of Ogwen Lake to a point between them over the crest of the buttress dividing Cwm Idwal from Cwm Bochlwyd. It is a narrow and rugged way but not beyond any walker, provided his head is not turned by the sweep downwards on either side at one point. From the toothy nature of this reef it is aptly called *Y Gribin*—the Hay-rake.

Clyd, Idwal, and Bochlwyd are all wild lakes which have never been tampered with by man. This can also be said of the lonely marsh pool right on the crest of the ridge called *Llyn Caseg Fraith*—Lake of the Dapple-grey Mare (in poetic balance with the Lake of the Stallion at the other extremity of the chain). The 2,500 foot contour runs by the margin. From here one looks down into Cwm Tryfan and towards the great semi-detached peak of that name which rises between it and Cwm Bochlwyd. The summit of *Tryfan* (3,010 feet) is not difficult to reach from the shore of Bochlwyd Lake, and the shortest way to Bochlwyd is the obvious one beside the fall which issues from it, but the more interesting way is to go up the track from Ogwen Cottage to Idwal Lake and on to Bochlwyd, first following the stream by the wall. This is a longer round but easier going and you have a lovelier surprise view of the upper lake.

Continuing the walk along the ridge from the Pool of the Dapple-grey Mare it is an easy descent along the gently falling watershed to Capel Curig, where a bridge on the old disused turnpike road of 1805 takes you over the River Llugwy into the village.

ACROSS THE RANGE

As already mentioned, an old pack-horse track (now only traceable in places) winds up from the lower end of Nant Ffrancon to the dip in the skyline called *Bwlch-y-Brecan*. A more direct approach to the gap is to make your way up the brow behind Maes Caradoc Farm, on the old road, keeping to the right of the stream, when a gate in the wire fence will be found and the open mountain reached. The stream comes from the hollow called *Cwm Perfedd*, a gentle, roomy place, as grassy as its next door neighbour, Cwm Graianog, is raw and stony. It must have been the pleasantest of all the summer-pastures in the old days when the farmer migrated with his beasts to his upland *hafod*. The remains of that house can still be seen. Near it is one of the only two rocking-stones I have ever heard of in Wales. The other, on the Great Orme's Head, which has been a little doctored and had a brass name-plate fixed to it, is not much more impressive. Both are quite small compared with the famous ones of Dartmoor and Cornwall. The Cwm Perfedd specimen probably doesn't weigh much above a ton, but it has had no publicity at all until now which is a point of interest in its favour.

From Bwlch-y-Brecan there is a long, smooth, even monotonous descent to Nant Peris with no well-marked path, but the stream is sufficient guide and will bring you down to the village of Old Llanberis.

It has been mentioned that there is an easy way up from Cwm Idwal to the plateau at the foot of Glyder Fawr. It starts from near the bottom of the Devil's Kitchen and is well marked by cairns. A path from Llyn-y-Cwn (shown on M.) leads down to the lower entrance of the Pass of Llanberis and from the south side of Glyder Fawr there is an easy way down to *Llyn Cwm-y-Ffynnon* which is just above the Gorphwysfa Hotel at the head of the Pass.

A much less arduous way of crossing the upper part of the range, between Nant Ffrancon and Nant-y-Benglog, than the rough track up the Gribin is to go from Bochlwyd Lake to the dip between Glyder Fach and Tryfan. From here a well-marked path can be seen leading round the cliffs of Cwm Tryfan up to the skyline. This brings you out near the pool of Caseg Fraith. There is a path from there to Pen-y-Gwryd.

On the range, itself, there are no *antiquities* to point out. Remains of at least two *cists* in Nant-y-Benglog give a clue to some population in the Bronze Age, while in Nant Ffrancon, in the field behind Saron Chapel at Tyn-y-Maes, are a pair of faintly marked *hut-circles* which probably recall a family residence of the Late Iron Age. From that little raised plateau they must have looked out over a birch-wood thicket covering the great flat marsh through which the Ogwen now flows, the stumps of whose trees still remain embedded in the peat.

A most surprising discovery has recently been made at Pen-y-Gwryd. It is the remains of a large four-square earthwork bestriding both roads just below the point where they fork. It is believed to be of

Roman origin—a temporary *fort* similar to those found near Hadrian's Wall which have been known as 'marching camps'.

Dolbadarn Castle (now under the guardianship of the Ministry of Works) is just outside the Park boundary, which runs between Old and New Llanberis, but the *parish church* is within it. It is mainly a fourteenth century building with later additions which have caused it to assume a curious and unusual shape. The framing of the old rood-screen with modern tracery is now at the west end of the church. The well of St. Peris is in a field across the road and is one of the best preserved, having been much visited for healing and wishing down to fairly recent times. It is one of those believed to foretell the fulfilment or otherwise of folks' desires by the behaviour of a sacred fish, and various writers, from Pennant in the eighteenth century downwards, mention the mysterious presence of a trout there. I can verify that when I visited the well in 1947 with a gift of some ground-bait the sacred fish did indeed appear. The old church at Capel Curig is seldom used and generally kept locked (key at the Vicarage at the cross-roads).

Snowdon

Snowdon is not only the highest, it is also the most distinctive of all the Welsh mountains, and in more ways than one. From the broad platform of Anglesey one may look back over the Menai Straits and see the whole of the northern ranges marshalled along the horizon from Penmaenmawr to the Rivals—a rugged sky-line of thirty-four miles. Snowdon stands in the midst, yet quite detached, its shape more comely than the rest. It looks, every inch, the complete mountain—there is no mistaking it! Looked straight down on from the air it is seen to be so much more compact in plan than its neighbours—a star-like lay-out. The summit is centrally placed on a noble peak supported, as it were, by five flying buttresses of rock, three of them knife-edge reefs with precipices on either hand, rising up from the east, south-east, and south-west, the other two extending at greater length to the north-west and north.

This striking configuration gives the mountain a scale of grandeur that makes it appear pre-eminent from distant points of view on all sides no less than at close quarters and, although in height it only beats Carnedd Llewelyn by a mere 76 feet, the unobscured range of outlook from the top exceeds that of any other summit. No wonder that the Welsh have always regarded Snowdon with a certain mystical reverence—a protective spirit, a symbol of fortitude and long continuance.

PLATE X (*a*). Glyder Fach, looking towards the summit of Glyder Fawr

PLATE X (*b*). Tryfan from Tal-y-braich farm

PLATE XI (b). The south aspect of Snowdon seen over
Llyn Llydaw

PLATE XI (a). The north aspect of Snowdon seen over
Llyn Padarn

The three clefts which give Snowdon its characteristic isolation are the Passes of Llanberis (to the east) (Plate XII a), Nant Gwynant (to the south), and Llyn Cwellyn (to the west). The latter has always lacked a recognized name either in English or, stranger still, in Welsh—for there is hardly an insignificant gap in the hills or the crossing of a watershed which has not been given an individual name as a *bwlch* (pass). So, for that picturesque corridor through the mountains followed by the Caernarvon-Beddgelert road, I borrow the name of its most conspicuous feature which is the large and fair lake, and call it the Pass of Llyn Cwellyn.

THE ASCENTS

It is one of the particular charms of Snowdon that the numerous ways to reach its summit are marked with so much variety both as to scenery and ease in walking. There are at least six beaten tracks, of which the least laborious and most completely free of any element of danger or excitement sets forth from *Llanberis*. It is certainly the dullest, but in Victorian times, when Welsh ponies and their attendant boys were available on three of the ascents, it was much the most popular, and the old pony trail is still well marked. In 1896 the Mountain Railway was made. It followed the pony-track; and now, if the mists descend, you can follow the railway and be certain of reaching your destination safely. The distance is about five miles.

From *Pen-y-Pass*, at the head of the Pass of Llanberis, there are three ways to choose from, all beginning opposite the Gorphwysfa Hotel. The first is a tolerably well-metalled cart-track, made for the copper-mines (now disused) about a century and a half ago. It follows a break in the declivity of the south-east face of Snowdon where two lakes lie, the small *Llyn Teyrn* and the large *Llyn Llydaw*, which is over a mile long. On the left, the ground rolls down to the brow overlooking the Pass of Nant Gwynant. Crossing the lake on a causeway, the track comes immediately under the foot of one of those 'knife-edged reefs' just mentioned, which abut on the central peak. Its jagged crest can be seen high in air and is aptly called *Crib Goch*—the Red Comb. A similar spur, with a theatrically jagged skyline and a still more precipitous face, stands right across the view beyond the head of the lake. This is *Lliwedd*. It abuts on the other side of the peak which, in another moment, can be seen standing very grandly over an upper hollow, from whose lip tumbles a waterfall.

Up to that shelf the track ascends—or what is left of it through long disuse, and there, another lake is discovered, *Glaslyn*. Formerly, the Welsh, like the ancient Greeks, seemed to have considered the

colour green as just a variant of blue and used the same word for both—
glas. And the water in this lake could well be described by either of
those border-line terms, peacock-blue or sea-green. Exactly the same
could be said of its river, the Glaslyn, which flows through the Pass
of that name. That rich veins of copper lace the rocks whence come the
springs to fill this lake is plain from the ruins of old mine workings
along its shore. Whether this is sufficient to tint the waters I have
never been able to find out, but I am certain that it is no mere accident
of light or reflection that gives them that vivid colour.

From the far shore of Glaslyn there rises the great precipice,
Clogwyn-y-Garnedd, which culminates in the pyramidal peak of the
mountain top, over a thousand and a half feet above, that feature that
never failed to stir the hearts of bards and patriots, the Summit Rock
with its special name *Y Wyddfa*. The cairn marking the highest 'spot'
is just out of sight but its presence is kept in mind through the precipice
being called 'of-the-Cairn' (y-Garnedd)—a nice point of sentiment.
The cairn has been so much made up and trampled on that you would
hardly recognize it as a sacred site and an ancient monument. Yet the
core of it goes back to prehistoric days. In legend it is spoken of as
chief of all the cairns on the mountain tops, marking the grave of the
most powerful of all the Welsh giants, Rhita Gawr.

To one side of the Clogwyn is a hollow which has rendered possible
the cutting of a zig-zag path up to the sky-line. If you ascend this it
brings you out on the ridge called *Crib-y-Ddisgl* which is the short
link between Crib Goch and Y Wyddfa. This zig-zag path is pretty
steep and rough for a man on foot. Yet not a century ago Welsh ponies
were regularly carrying tourists up it.

The *Pig Track*[1] also starts from Pen-y-Pass a few yards further
to the north than the other. It is a well-marked but rough footpath
and very wet in one place. It takes a line two or three hundred feet above
the cart-track and brings one directly to the spring of Crib Goch Ridge.
A clear branch to the right takes one up to the crest of the ridge and so
on to Crib-y-Ddysgl and the Summit. It is rough going but not
dangerous in fair weather.

From the turning to the ascent of Crib Goch the Pig Track goes on
towards Glaslyn. It reaches the hollow about 300 feet above the level
of the lake and makes its way round to join the zig-zag path. It is a
shorter and wilder approach than the Cart Track though more arduous.
Its chief advantage lies in the views to be had along it, especially those

---

[1] The name seems to be quite obviously derived from a gap in a spur through
which the path goes called *Bwlch Moch*—the Pig's Gap, though the modern map
has now changed the spelling to Pyg on the assumption, it would seem, that the
name was derived from the initial letters of Pen-y-Gwryd.

of the great shaggy rock curtain of Lliwedd drawn across the end of Lake Llydaw, which lies some four or five hundred feet below.

Lliwedd, like Crib Goch, is a knife-edge with a precipice on either hand and a cock's comb crest, along which, in the same manner one can walk and scramble. It is easily accessible at its southern end below the lake and affords another means of reaching the Summit. These two ridges which make a wide embrace about the lakes, form between them what is called *The Horseshoe*. To go up one way and come down the other is now one of the most popular ways of 'doing' Snowdon. But the elderly stranger who is not in training form is not advised to try it.

The *Watkin Ascent* (which has the most curious history of all) starts between the two lakes, Gwynant and Dinas, in the middle of the Pass of Nant Gwynant. The name has no connection with the famous Welsh family of Wynnstay but recalls one of the most magnificent schemers of the Railway Age, Sir Edward Watkin. The son of a Manchester cotton merchant, he dreamed of making a railway from Manchester to Paris. In this he nearly succeeded. By gaining control of existing companies in the north and south and building a long inter-vening link on his own initiative (which later became the Great Central Railway) he contrived to run his trains from Manchester to Dover and then set to work on the Channel Tunnel. He had proceeded for nearly a mile underground on either side of the Straits when a timid Government stopped his operations. When he was seventy years of age his tired but still romantic spirit was attracted by the sublime image of Snowdon. He acquired the choicest of all spots at its foot and there built The Chalet in the woods between the Lakes and within sound of the waterfalls of Cwm-y-Llan. It was natural that after his ambitious projects in transportation he should wish to provide some means of getting from his own front door to the top of the mountain. Accordingly, he had a respectable path constructed from the South Snowdon Slate quarries, where the cart road ended, to the western side of the Lliwedd Ridge and on through the *Bwlch-y-Saethau* to join the Beddgelert path close to the summit.

The Watkin Ascent, though much less frequented than it used to be, is still the most romantic, rising as it does from a sheltered valley of luxuriant vegetation, fine trees, thickets of rhododendron, and en-chanting waterfalls. The path was opened in 1892 by Sir Edward Watkin's guest W. E. Gladstone, then Prime Minister. The spot where he stood to deliver the inaugural address is duly marked on the rock and on the map.

On the western side of Snowdon there are two well marked ways. One has always been known as the *Beddgelert Track* though it leaves the road more than two miles away from the village. The other begins at Snowdon Ranger, a house opened as an inn in the early nineteenth century by a mountain guide who gave it this unique sign and doubtless blazed the original trail. Later, it became a monastery, and is now a Youth Hostel. *The Snowdon Ranger Path* is the easier of the two to walk and the less sensational. The Beddgelert Track starts from the lane leading to Ffridduchaf, opposite Pitt's Head, and reserves a thrill for the walker at the end of his journey. Here it crosses the *Bwlch Main* which is the third knife-edge ridge having a long steep descent on either side—a *bwlch* (pass) in reverse.

On any day of the year, no matter what the season or the weather, it is seldom that one is quite alone on any of the fore-going trails. But off these well beaten routes there is much of Snowdon that is unfrequented. Not often is the little wild, shallow pool, *Llyn Glas*, which lies deep in the craggy fastnesses of the south-east corner visited, or the country eastward of the long north-west spur—except the cliffs about the fearsome hollow above *Llyn Du'r-Arddu*, famous for all kinds of rockclimbing. But this hollow is the wildest thing on Snowdon. There are two ways across the north-west spur into the Pass of Llanberis, the more direct branching off from the Snowdon Ranger Path and leading to Llanberis through the gap on the south side of *Foel Goch*. The last considerable hill in the spur, *Moel Eilio* (2,363 feet), has always been held to command some of the finest and most interesting views in Wales.

The Pass of Llyn Cwellyn. The group of hills to the west of this pass, when seen from Anglesey, appears like an elephant lying down with its forehead towards Snowdon. The resemblance can still be seen at closer quarters as you approach from Caernarvon. The beast is formed by the mountain *Mynydd Mawr* (2,291 feet) and its head by an astonishing excrescence called *Craig Cwm Bychan*. But it has, from the earliest days of Welsh guide-books, enjoyed the English name of the *Elephant Mountain*. Craig Cwm Bychan is a very striking mass of rock and, confronting Moel Eilio, it makes a most impressive portal not only to this Pass but also to the Park, whose boundary lies just beyond the church of Betws Garmon (a dedication recalling St. Germanus). At Rhyd-ddu a road turns off to go down to the coast through the Pass of *Drws-y-Coed* (Plate XII b) between the off-side of the Elephant Mountain and the high ridge that forms the upper limit of the Hebog Range. The watershed is another mile further on and has a natural landmark in the shape of a huge erratic boulder. In its profile some traveller in the early part of the last century saw a likeness to the then Prime Minister, William Pitt, the younger. This gave it notoriety above all other erratics and put it on the map as *Pitt's Head*.

NANT GWYNANT

The two lakes, Gwynant and Dinas (Plate XIII a), formed in the course of the River Glaslyn are the principal features. Their shape and setting among native woodlands and great rock masses of singular beauty give this pass a claim to first rank in natural scenery. It possesses, too, some interesting antiquities. In the upper valley above Lake Gwynant there is a group of hut-circles—a settlement that may have been in existence when the Romans set about building their fort at the head of the pass, overlooking it (page 69); if so, it is not difficult to imagine the feelings of those villagers.

Near Llyn Gwynant is the well-preserved old Welsh homestead, *Hafod Lwyfog*, dated 1638, marking the reconstruction of an earlier house—the one in which Sir John Williams was born, who became goldsmith to James I. He presented his old parish church of Beddgelert with a splendid chalice bearing his name and the date 1610. It is still in use. The house and its land were given to the National Trust in 1938 by Mr. Clough Williams-Ellis.

But the most truly romantic thing is the little pointed, detached hill below Llyn Dinas called *Dinas Emrys*. It is associated in tradition with Merlyn and Vortigern, that unhappy British King of Kent who is credited with being the first to give the land-hungry Anglo-Saxons an excuse for entering Britain. Whether or not Vortigern did beat a retreat to this remote spot, it is true enough that some fine pieces of Late Iron Age equipment have been found here. And whether or not he built a castle here under Merlin's instructions (as the story goes) there are sure signs that some prince of the twelfth century certainly did.

Before the old wide estuary of the Glaslyn was reclaimed by the building of the embankment at Portmadoc, shipping could come up to the bridge at Pont Aberglaslyn. Overland routes from here to Caernarvon and Bangor saved weathering the formidable headlands of the Lleyn Peninsula and the race in the Sound of Bardsey, and in the Middle Ages, Beddgelert was busy as a seaport. A Celtic monastery was established here in the sixth century. These monks of the native Church were superseded in the late twelfth or early thirteenth by canons of the Augustinian Order, whose church now serves the parish. It retains two of its ancient features, the fine triple lancet windows at the east end and an arcade on the north side, both of thirteenth century work. I think this is not the place to tell or to spoil the story of Gelert's grave.

The Hebog Range

Moel Hebog—the Mountain of the Hawk—cuts a fine bold figure over Beddgelert (Plate XIII a) and looks twice its measured height. It is the highest member of the range which is composed of two chains of hills nearly at right angles to each other. From south to north, overlooking the Beddgelert-Caernarvon road, the principals are *Moel-ddu* (1,811 feet), *Moel Hebog* (2,566 feet), *Moel Lefn* (2,094 feet). These are round-headed eminences, as their names *moel* (bald) imply—the dumpings of lava and ash from the old Snowdon volcano. Then comes a dip in the skyline where the ancient road into the Pennant Valley crossed the ridge at the *Bwlch-y-ddwy-elor*—the Pass-of-two-biers—and then the great corner-stone, *Mynydd Drws-y-Coed*, where the range turns to go from east to west.

The pass just mentioned is a tell-tale name, recalling the days when a funeral proceeded from one valley to the other, and the mourners bore their dead on the parish bier up the long rough path to the watershed which divided the parishes. There they were met by a party bringing the bier of their own church to complete the journey.

Mynydd Drws-y-Coed stands over the village of Rhyd-ddu where the branch road turns off to go down into the Vale of Nantlle through the once thickly wooded pass which gives its name to the mountain, *Drws-y-Coed*, the Door-of-the-wood. The opposite side of the pass is formed by an imposing flank of the Elephant Mountain. Just at the entrance to the defile is the lake, *Llyn Dywarchen*, which has attracted attention at various times since the twelfth century (when it was noted by Giraldus Cambrensis) through the freak of possessing a floating island. This only happens when part of the peaty margin detaches itself and drifts off. It is not a regular event and visitors are warned against disappointment.

The aspect of the western chain of heights is as different as possible from the other. Instead of solidly rounded forms it is a series of crests sharply cut round the rims of huge hollows like split craters. Craig Cwm Silyn (2,408 feet) the midmost and highest crag is marked by a large circular cairn which in distant views looks like a round tower.

The range covers a large area whose greatest length is nine miles, and breadth, seven. It is penetrated by a single valley which opens at its lowest fringe on the south-west and is closed by a vast, imposing hollow just inside the elbow where the two chains of mountains join. This is the Pennant Valley famous for both its beauty and its folklore (for there are families still living here who claim descent from the fairies). Its landscape features are as near perfect as one could imagine. Following up the River Dwyfor from the entrance, the first note, a dramatic one, is struck by a reef of dark igneous rock which thrusts itself across the way, forcing road and river into a gorge at the foot of which is the tiny church of Llanfihangel-y-Pennant. Thereafter, the valley opens out to a wide, grassy *ystrad* (strath), and one sees on either hand gentle slopes rising to the heights of those outer escarpments as they converge towards the great precipitous hollow and its dominant peak at the head of the valley and from which its name is drawn—Cwm Pennant. It is a skyline wonderfully balanced (as already observed) by a cresting both round-headed and aquiline.

ASCENT OF MOEL HEBOG

The short way is very straightforward. You take the lane to Cwm Cloch Farm, either by turning into it over the bridge just above Beddgelert or by the branch lane which starts behind the Goat Hotel. Beyond Cwm Cloch, the sign on the corner of an outhouse indicates the footpath to the mountain gate, whence you may follow your nose or the numerous cairns right up to the top with only one very modest scramble at a point packed with geological bombs, the well preserved relics of an ancient volcanic bombardment.

The top, which is quite flat, but punctuated by two cairns, looks out on the opposite side over a long slope, as gentle as the one just climbed was abrupt. A descent on that side, guided by eye, will take you to the Portmadoc-Caernarvon road in about six miles. In doing this you may strike one of several lane-ends. But to ascend from this side the best approach is to take the road into the Pennant Valley and turn off it by the chapel above Llanfihangel-y-Pennant. Then make for the mountain.

The next eminence to Moel Hebog, on the northern side of the ridge, is an astonishing rock, riven on its eastern face with deep horizontal clefts, the largest of which goes by the name of *Ogof Owain Glyndwr*—Owen Glendower's Cave. There is a strong tradition that the great national hero took refuge here from his English pursuers in one of the difficult intervals of his campaign. Its utter wildness today sustains the romance of the story. Plantations of the Forestry Commission have made it difficult to reach, but it can be visited on the third and most attractive of the approaches to Moel Hebog.

This begins at Rhyd-ddu at a right-angled bend in the road to Nantlle, just above the village. There are two iron gates on the left hand side, the smaller opening on the old footpath to Cwm Pennant, not used so much as formerly and consequently less well marked. It leads to a small gate in a wall bounding the Forestry Commission plantation, across which the track must be followed. It emerges on the high ground and crosses the watershed at the Pass-of-two-biers, descending on the far side of the mountain wall to Cwm Pennant and Dolbenmaen. It is here that you must break off and make your way along the ridge towards Moel Hebog which almost immediately comes into full view.

From the same little gate above Rhyd-ddu, and bearing more to the right, one can reach *Y Garn* (2,080 feet) the highest point of Mynydd-Drws-y-Coed, from whence one may hug that sharp northern skyline of half-craters and knife-edges to the last high point, *Garnedd Goch* (2,301 feet), and so down to the main road at Llanllyfni, but it is rough and strenuous going.

ANTIQUITIES

The boundary of the Park cuts obliquely across country from Llanberis to a point on the Caernarvon–Criccieth road where it makes a descent to Pant Glas. From thence it follows round the skirt of the Hebog Range and encloses the whole of that interesting region. Near the point (just mentioned) where the Park boundary joins the road there stand three enormous gate-posts. They are re-used prehistoric monoliths (one has been riven to make two posts). The larger was brought from over a mile away with a team of nine horses within living memory. Near them, on land belonging to *Caerau Farm* is a large settlement of which so far (1958) only a few houses have been excavated indicating a date of 3rd–4th century A.D. It borders the road, and the old cultivation terraces mounting up the hillside are plainly marked.

This part is rich in prehistoric remains, including the fine cromlechs of Cefn-isaf and Ystum Cegid, but they lie outside the Park. Three early Christian tombstones, all ascribed to the sixth century, are also here. One is at *Llystyn-gwyn Farm*, near Brynkir, only a few yards outside the boundary. It is of particular interest as having an ogham as well as a Latin inscription (the only ogham in North Wales) but it is hard to make out. Another is in Treflys churchyard. The third is at *Gesail-gyfarch*, near Penmorfa. This is well within the Park boundary. It lies in the farm garden and commemorates one Cunacus, son of Cunalipus.

There are old parish churches at *Llanllyfni* (with a much neglected saint's well in a field nearby, *Dolbenmaen*, and *Penmorfa*. The latter, with its saddle-roof lych-gate dated 1698 and memorial to the doughty royalist veteran, Sir John Owen, is the most interesting. By the farm opposite Dolbenmaen Church is a large motte mound. This, with its small wooden castle was probably the seat of the rulers of the district— the Lords of Eifionydd—in the twelfth century, before they removed to Cricceth.

Tremadoc takes its name from that enterprising private person W. A. Madocks who spent his fortune on reclaiming the wide estuary of the Glaslyn by building the sea wall at Portmadoc (completed, 1812). The little town with its church, market square, and combined market-hall and theatre was all laid out and built by him about 1805.

PLATE XII (*a*). The Pass of Llanberis, from Pen-y-Pass

PLATE XII (*b*). The Pass of Drws-y-Coed, Hebog Range

PLATE XIII (*a*). Moel Hebog and Llyn Dinas

PLATE XIII (*b*). Moel Siabod and River Llugwy

PLATE XIV (*a*). Maentwrog, Vale of Ffestiniog

PLATE XIV (*b*). The Rhinogs from Trawsfynydd-Dolgelley Road

PLATE XV. The Roman Steps, Cwm Bychan, the Rhinogs

THE COED TREMADOC (TREMADOC WOOD) NATURE RESERVE

This is situated on the great rocky escarpment which dominates the town and the road leading thence to Beddgelert where a dense growth of oak clothes the precipitous face right up to the skyline. Formerly, oak woodland was one of the principal scenic glories of North Wales but in recent years it has suffered greatly either through absolute clearance or replacement by coniferous plantations. Its conservation here where it has always made a particularly important contribution to the landscape will be welcomed by all lovers of natural beauty. Apart from that, the reserve has an interesting botany partly owing to its rock formation and the fact that its steepness has prevented the ubiquitous all-nibbling sheep from reaching ledges where rare plants have had a chance of survival. But, unlike the other two, a *permit* is necessary to enter this reserve. For that, an application should be made to The Nature Conservancy, Y Fron, The Crescent, Upper Bangor, Bangor, Caernarvonshire: Telephone Bangor 512.

The Siabod and Moelwyn Range

This lies at the feet of all four ranges described—a footstool with its axis at right angles to theirs. It contains two mountains whose features are notable contributions to landscape—*Moel Siabod* in the east and *Cnicht* in the west—otherwise its distinction lies not in its interior scenery but in the number and beauty of the passes and valleys which it both helps to form and to dominate. Going the round anti-clockwise from Betws-y-Coed, there is the Llugwy Valley (below the Carnedd Range), Nant-y-Gwryd (below the Glyders), Nant Gwynant (below Snowdon), the narrow Pass of Aber Glaslyn at the foot of Moel Hebog, followed by the wide expanse of Traeth Mawr, the reclaimed estuary, whose sands and channels are replaced by a broad green interlude starred with the gold of gorse; then the well-wooded and rightly famous Vale of Ffestiniog, then up on to a high pass on the open mountain at a thousand feet properly called Bwlch Gorddinan but now generally known as *Crimea* after the sign of a long vanished inn. Down, then into the lovely Lledr Valley, then to a short stretch of the Upper Conway where, in a deep gap, the bastions of four ranges confront one another, divided by four remarkable valleys. Through one, high up, above the Conway Falls, Telford's Holyhead road comes and, at one turning, gives the west-bound traveller a sudden and most astonishing view over the deep gap. He sees, as it were, the very essence of Snowdonia at a glance— a highly modelled foreground of rocks, woods, and waters with a broad mountain plinth rising above and, on it, the blue silhouette of Moel

Siabod couched like a sharp-featured sphinx. Before the native oak and birch were replaced by conifers this was one of the most wonderful views in the whole of the British Isles.

Moel Siabod is a solitary mountain with smooth grassy slopes which rise evenly above the Mymbyr Lakes and *Nant-y-Gwryd* on its northern flank and its long back sloping upwards from the west, but it presents a rough and rugged front to the south-east, immediately below its summit (2,860 feet). Here it has been hollowed by its old glacier to an amphitheatre filled with relics of that time—round drumlin mounds and a lake, *Llyn-y-Foel*, with its island of morainic detritus and large boulders. That 'plinth' just mentioned extends on this side in the form of a large plateau nearly a thousand feet up, from the heights above Betws-y-Coed to the sources of the Lledr River above Dolwyddelan.

From the Holyhead Road, between Capel Curig and Betws-y-Coed, the mountain is seen to stand boldly against the sky in the form of a pyramid and it is from this side that the most attractive approach is made.

ASCENTS OF MOEL SIABOD

By crossing the River Llugwy at *Pont Cyfyng*, a mile below Capel Curig, you come to a terrace of houses. Behind them is the end of a rough road which served the now disused slate quarries and one or two hill farms. This leads directly to the foot of the mountain on its rough side. It begins by a ridge with curving bands of strongly marked strata, the intervals forming gulleys not difficult to make one's way up and by so doing reach the summit. A more interesting alternative is to continue along the road which leads past the upper quarry with its artificial pools and ruined buildings to the wild lake in the hollow. From here the summit can be reached by making one's way up the middle gulley or the boulder-strewn edge of the cirque.

From Capel Curig there is a path up the all-grassy slope which starts opposite the end of the bridge by *Plas-y-Brenin*. This is now the hostel of the Central Council of Physical Recreation (page 35), formerly the Royal Hotel. It was built to serve the earlier turnpike road to Holyhead and opened in 1804. Its window-panes bear signatures of Byron, Walter Scott, and Queen Victoria. A plantation of the Forestry Commission bestrides the old path which is no longer well marked at the upper end, but by keeping near the wire fence on the right when the trail becomes doubtful a stile on to the open mountain will be found. This is the shortest and easiest way up. Besides the cairn on the summit there is a small circular enclosure. It was a pen for ponies which brought tourists up the mountain in earlier days.

The high plateau, which sweeps round the base of Moel Siabod from a point overlooking the Conway gorge in the east to another some 10 miles to the west overlooking Gwynant Lake, has a conspicuous building nearly mid-way which can be seen from far off in all directions. This is *Dolwyddelan Castle*, its rectangular keep reminding one of the peel towers of Scotland and Ireland. Built in the twelfth century, it is believed on good grounds to have been the birthplace of Llewelyn the Great (1173). In 1488 Maredydd ap Ivan, ancestor of the Wynns of Gwydir, acquired the castle and migrated here from the ancient family home at Cesail-gyfarch. He built old *Dolwyddelan Church* in the early sixteenth century, which still preserves its rood-screen and some old glass of his time. Maredydd was the grandfather of John Wynn who built Gwydir Castle, Llanrwst, and great grandfather of the more famous Sir John.

The castle stands near the junction of two ancient routes. Down Cwm Penmaen (opposite the modern village of Dolwyddelan) came the Roman road from Tomen-y-mur called Sarn Helen. It must have crossed the plateau to the fort at Caer Llugwy (page 63) though its exact route has not yet been ascertained. From Nant Gwynant came another road which passed under its battlements. M. shows this as 'Ancient Trackway' but though the direction indicated makes an excellent walk the old trail is now obliterated throughout most of its length. That the plateau was more popular as a resort in both the Iron Age and the Bronze Age is shown by groups of hut-circles and, in the eastern part, cist-burials.

South of the 'Ancient Trackway' which is like the waist-line of the range the ground rises towards the extraordinary mountain complex dotted with more than two dozen lakes and tarns, with round-headed *Moelwyn Mawr* (2,527 feet) as chief summit, and sharp-featured *Cnicht* (2,265 feet) the most striking as seen from below.

The best entry into this country, which has a singular charm of its own and commands some unrivalled views, is to branch off the 'Ancient Trackway' and follow the stream up *Cwm Edno* to the lake of that name. It is rather more than two miles from there to Cnicht and another two miles on to Moelwyn Mawr. Cnicht is actually an elongated ridge, the gable end of which gives it the appearance of a peak from below where, in fact, it resembles the shape of the bascinet helmet of a knight of the fourteenth century (then spelt *cnight* and pronounced with a gutteral *gh*) so, most likely, it is an English and not a Welsh name given by sailors frequenting the estuary of the Glaslyn before reclamation converted its channels into green pastures.

9

Meirion

The Rhinogs

BETWEEN Moelwyn, at the end of the Siabod group, and Cader Idris, at the end of the Berwyn chain, is a range of coastal mountains almost at right angles to both and facing squarely to the west. It is generally known by the name of the two sister mountains which confront each other on either side of the principal pass through the middle of the range—Rhinog Fawr (2,362 feet) and Rhinog Fach (2,333 feet). They are not the highest but they are the most distinctive, Rhinog Fawr cutting a tower-like figure with a flat top sloped to the west and snubbed off to the east, the other having a slight sisterly resemblance.

The whole region is markedly different from Snowdonia. The shapes of the mountains, the more luxurious vegetation, the ways of the people all impress one as individual and indigenous. It was, in ancient days, the separate district of Ardudwy, whose chief appears to have had two royal residences, one on the rock of Harlech, the other in the deserted Roman castellum of Tomen-y-mur.

The range is particularly well off for lakes still in their natural state. The most beautiful of these is *Llyn Cwm Bychan* where some fine hardwood timber gives it that touch of richness generally lacking in the mountain lakes of Wales. Other touches are the purple *cwm* rising behind the woodland to the peak of Pen-y-clip; the noble Careg-y-saeth—Crag of the Arrow—scored with bilberry and heather terraces, standing sheer in the south bank and throwing its shadow and reflection on the water; the single dwelling, a white farmstead, for centuries the home of the Lloyds of Cwm Bychan. By contrast, there is *Llyn Hywel*, sunk in between Rhinog Fach and *Y Llethr* (2,475 feet, the highest of the range) the most stark and forbidding of all the mountain tarns in the Park—quite a frightening place!

The hills north of the pass called *Drws Ardudwy*—the Door of Ardudwy—are a compact group with mainly rounded summits rising from a breadth of high ground and culminating in Rhinog Fawr. Their slopes are covered with deep heather, and large expanses of rock-face tend to be lined by ledges and terraces where heather and bilberry grow luxuriantly. Moist hollows are crammed with the fragrant bog-myrtle and, in the valleys of the western slopes, ferns flourish abundantly.

South of the pass, characteristics tend to grow more austere, and the main watershed becomes a single elongated ridge stretching from Y Llethr to the headland above Barmouth (some nine miles), embracing on the west side a wide upland plateau, once, and for long, a much favoured resort of man, for it is covered with the signs of occupation, from the Neolithic period down to the last phase of the Iron Age. From about the middle of this ridge a spur extends due east to the Vale of Ganllwyd forming a watershed which sends a number of streams due south to the Mawddach estuary, their pleasant sunny valleys, *Cwm Sylfaen*, *Hirgwm*, *Cwm Mynach*, and *Cwm yr Winn*, open on the Barmouth–Dolgelley road. The highest point achieved by the spur is *Y Garn* (2,063 feet).

THE SURROUNDING COUNTRY

In the north, the range is bounded by the famous Vale of Ffestiniog, whose beauty is still enriched by deciduous woodlands through which the River Dwyryd winds down to the village of Maentwrog (Plate XIV a) —the Stone of Twrog. That stone is evidently the monolith standing near the tower of the much modernised church. It recalls the sixth century missioner, a close companion of the more noted Beuno. The stone bears no inscription and may conceivably have been there when Twrog arrived to found the first Christian church—a prehistoric memorial marking a pagan sacred site.

To the east, the range is completely detached from the neigh-bouring *Migneint* by the wide valley which takes such a direct course from north to south that the Ffestiniog–Dolgelley road is almost in a dead straight line for several miles. From the long stretch of open moorland and peat-bog the road descends into the thickly wooded Vale of Ganllwyd (now mainly converted from native timber to conifer), then turns to the west and, at Llanelltyd bridge, meets the tidal waters of the Mawddach estuary. From here to Barmouth the road winds between the shore and the foot of those valleys just mentioned. It is along this southern edge of the range that the gold-bearing reef runs which has been worked by various undertakings with considerable profit, though at the present time (1958) all the mines are closed down. Fittingly enough, the scenery along this tortuous highway has a poetically golden quality, too. Natural woodlands abound, with slopes of heather and gorse intervening; the shore-line is fretted with headlands and sedgy pools; there are constant glimpses across the water towards the majestic front of Cader Idris.

On the western side of the range, the foothills do not rise directly to the shore but form a fringe of low-lying fertile land between which and the sea a long barrier of sandhills projects. To this feature is owed the long-standing name *Dyffryn Ardudwy*, where the normal use of the word 'dyffryn', 'a valley', is extended to convey the meaning of good land between the barrenness of mountain and sea. The name is significant in this particular context, for one may believe that it is intended to include more than that mere fringe of fertile ground. Beyond the first rise above the road there is that ample plateau, mentioned above, which reaches right up into the hills and is bounded by the Llethr Ridge. Except for a couple of mountain farms, far apart from each other, it is only inhabited by sheep. Yet it is strewn with the remains of ancient populations. If you begin exploring at road level you will find a splendid pair of cromlechs in the playground of Dyffryn Ardudwy school. They are the exposed chambers of a Neolithic long barrow which has lost its enclosing mound. It is rare to find one which still retains any of its original covering, but such are the *Carneddau Hengwm*—shown on both the Ordnance and Bartholomew maps. There are other crom- lechs in a more ruinous condition. Above Cors-y-gedol you may catch glimpses through the bracken of round cairns in serried ranks—doubt- less a large Bronze Age cemetery. Their presence side-by-side with the larger tombs of the earlier period will account for at least a thousand years of settled life in the dyffryn. The place was yet again favoured by Celtic immigrants, for there are two Iron Age forts and innumerable hut-circles, which cartographers, glutted by so many 'ancient monu- ments', have not troubled to mark. That plateau can be likened to nowhere else this side of the Irish Sea but Salisbury Plain.

Probably it was a folk memory of the Old People of Hengwm which started the story of the Cantref-y-Gwaelod—the Hundred of the Sea- floor—the lost land overwhelmed through neglect of sea dykes, a tale fortified by the presence of an extraordinary submarine barrier of large loose stones extending in a straight line from the sandhills of Morfa Dyffryn for fourteen miles out to sea and called *Sarn Badrig*—Patrick's Causeway. Formerly believed to be artificial, it was an antiquarian problem; now held to be natural, it is one for the geologist, who has not yet produced a convincing solution.

On the north-west fringe of the range there are also prehistoric remains scattered about (many, doubtless, still unrecorded). A by-road going up steeply from Llanfair towards Moel Goedog passes the group of hut-circles marked on M. as *Muriau'r Gwyddelod*—Walls of the Goidels, i.e. the Irish-speaking people—then, further on, beside the rough track, three monoliths; *Moel Goedog* itself is crowned by an Iron Age fort. A reminder that these high places were still peopled in the sixth century is the parish church of *Llandecwyn*, founded by the missionary Tegwyn at that time at a height of 500 feet and remote from any modern settlement. On the extreme coastal fringe, too, parishioners have also moved away and *Llandanwg* church is now quite deserted among the outer sandhills, and the old congregation of *Llanfihangel-y-traethau* has migrated to newer settlements on the main road, but the church is worth visiting for the charm of its situation and the remarkable twelfth century pillar stone in the graveyard. Of the six other old parish churches, *Llanaber* is the most interesting and architecturally most unusual for Wales, being built in the Early English style, and is complete with clerestory. Two inscribed stones of the fifth or sixth century are preserved there (two of similar date are at Llandanwg). Still more rare is the monolith kept in *Llanbedr* church with a spiral picked out on it. No one knows who put it there or whence it came, but it can hardly be younger than the Bronze Age. Even more stimulating to conjecture is the much later stone in *Llanelltyd* church (twelfth century?) which bears the outline of a footprint and an inscription which has been translated as 'The footprint of Kenyric is affixed to the top of the stone and he himself is bound (by his vow made) before he set out on a journey' —a noble pilgrim? a crusader?

Harlech Castle (Plate VI) has its own excellent guide-book. In the modern church the mediaeval font of the older mother at Llandanwg will be found.

Barmouth (an old English malaprop for *Aber Maw*) is a very ancient seaport which was still commercially important in the first part of the nineteenth century when they had found it necessary to build the picturesque round house on the foreshore as a prison for rowdy mariners. The old town, built so steeply on the rock that the houses have no access by wheeled vehicle, is stranger and foreigner than the much more visited Clovelly. Among the cottages are several held by a trust founded by John Ruskin in 1871, and the first gift to the National Trust was four-and-a-half acres of the headland overlooking the town, made over to the Nation in 1895, called prophetically The Castle of Light, a beacon to which all National Parks must own guidance.

WAYS OVER THE RANGE

The Pass of Drws Ardudwy is the only way through for wheeled vehicles. Unlike most Welsh passes it is a gloomy place, but a fit setting for the house on the western side, *Maes-y-Garnedd*, and its associations. In the seventeenth century it was the home of Colonel John Jones who married Catherine, the sister of Oliver Cromwell. He had the misfortune to put his hand to the death-warrant of Charles I and then outlive the Commonwealth regime. At the Restoration he was awarded the traitor's death. On the rocks above the pass one may sometimes see the shaggy form of one or more members of the herd of naturalized goats.

From Cwm Bychan a paved pack-horse trail ascends to a high cleft in the mountain, called *Bwlch Tyddiad*. The path takes the form at intervals of a stairway with elongated treads which horses can use, and bears the traditional name of the *Roman Steps* (Plate XV). Sceptics name a seventeenth century date as more likely for their construction, when the Lloyds of Cwm Bychan were flourishing in the heart of their isolated domain. The mystery will probably remain non-proven, but it is likely that the route is a very ancient one and was not made exclusively for the convenience of Cwm Bychan House, for there are remains of it beyond the Farm going in the direction of Harlech, though this part is unused and has fallen entirely into ruin, while the rest is tolerably well preserved. The distance from the Farm to the Ffestiniog–Dolgelley road is about six miles. The farmers attending fairs and sheep-dog trials at Trawsfynydd have formed an alternative path which goes up through the head of the cwm and leads to the footbridge near the end of the hydro-electric reservoir.

The Roman Steps also provide an easy and attractive way to reach the summit of Rhinog Fawr (the general favourite, though not the highest of the Range). They may be left when *Llyn Morwynion*— Lake of the Maidens—comes into view, and the way over the open moorland is obvious and straightforward.

The old road from Dolgelley to Harlech surveyed by John Ogilby for his map published in 1675 turns off the present main road at Bontddu. It is metalled and maintained for about two miles and then becomes a mere track. This divides where an ancient milestone of Stuart date (it is shown in Ogilby's map) stands. It directs you straight forward for Tal-y-bont, and to the right for Harlech. Either way is full of interest. The way to Tal-y-bont (in full use till the lower road was made) goes through the head of Cwm Sylfaen, a valley with an individual charm of bold and simple contours, past the ruin of an ancient inn, and over the Llethr Ridge at the Pass of Rhiwgyr. This brings you on to the great plateau that was so full of life in prehistoric times but is so void of it now.

The old track to Harlech also crosses the ridge and reaches the plateau at a point about two miles higher up where it spans the river by a pack-horse bridge called *Pont Scethin*, remarkable for its isolation in a wild environment. Three lakes lie near it, the highest, a small wild gem, is right under the rocky escarpment where the Llethr Ridge turns to join the mountain of that name (highest of the range) by a knife-edge. North of these rocks there is a good approach to this summit and, south of them, a convenient way down into *Cwm Mynach* and the

PLATE XVI (*a*). Arenig Fawr, western aspect

PLATE XVI (*b*). Bala Lake, looking towards Aran Benllyn

PLATE XVII (*a*). The Mawddach Estuary and foothills of Cader Idris

PLATE XVII (*b*). The Talyllyn Railway, Dolgoch Viaduct

lane which leads back to the main road. That gap can of course be reached by sticking to the high ground of the Ridge instead of following the track down to Pont Scethin.

The Migneint and Arenig Region

This is a large and varied mountain group, better described as a region than a range. Its continuity is best illustrated by saying that you can enter it at Pentre Foelas (through which the eastern boundary of the Park passes) and go from thence to Dolgelley, a matter of nearly 30 miles, crossing only one public road (between the two Arenigs) in transit. Taking this walk, with only slight deviations from the straight line you could cross all the principal summits contained in the region, namely, *Carnedd-y-Filiast* (2,194 feet), *Arenig Fach* (2,264 feet), *Arenig Fawr* (2,800 feet), *Moel Llyfnant* (2,451 feet), *Y Dduallt* (2,155 feet), and *Rhobell Fawr* (2,408 feet).

'Migneint' is a convenient name for the northern sector of the region as it is marked prominently in capitals on all maps, though it only refers to a small part of it. The word means The Swampy Place. The hill, *Carnedd Iago* (1,765 feet)—The Cairn of James—is the spongy hub which gives rise to streams which radiate like spokes to all points of the compass. Most of them contribute to the Conway, though the source of that river is over three miles north of James's Cairn on a separate moorland plateau. It springs from Conway Lake, famous for its lusty trout and formerly strictly preserved by the Lords of Penrhyn.[1] Rising between gentle swelling breasts of moorland, with a surface level of 1,488 feet above the sea, its short course thither is fair in every part. In its earlier stage, a little below the head-waters, it is literally gilt-edged in the Spring with the lovely globe-flower. There follow the rapids in the defile crossed and re-crossed by the Holyhead Road, the Conway Falls, the Fairy Glen, the great salmon pools at the confluences of the Lledr and the Llugwy, the tree-shaded reaches of the Conway Valley, and then that noble estuary.

The country about Conway Lake belonged to the Knights of St. John of Jerusalem who had a preceptory at *Yspytty-Ifan*—The Hospital of John—of which the little parish church (rebuilt, 1858, but retaining some memorials) is the only reminder. Until the Dissolution of the Monasteries, the whole lordship of Yspyty was a sanctuary where the king's writ did not run and the rule of the Knights was not strong enough to prevent it becoming a den of thieves who terrorized the whole neighbourhood. One of the broken effigies in the church is of particular interest. It is that of Rhys ap Meredydd, who bore Henry Tudor's red dragon standard at the Battle of Bosworth.

[1] And still is, although now a National Trust property.

On a still more ancient site, at *Penmachno* in the adjoining valley, stands another brand new church. But within, or close by, are no less than five early Christian tombstones, four of them inscribed and of unusual interest. One has the sacred Chi-Rho monogram (Plate V b), another (Plate V a) is to 'a citizen of Venedos' (the early form of Gwynedd), a third mentions that it was set up in the time of the Roman consul Justinus.

Round Conway Lake and all over the Migneint, flocks of curlews come in the early Spring to found new families. The scent of ling and water-plants loading the clear air is set to music by the perpetual trills of their mating addresses. From here you look straight out on to the sturdy forms of the Arenigs, a tender azure or violent purple according to the weather. Less exciting is the outline of Carnedd-y-Filiast[1] and those of its neighbours due east—though geologically related to the Arenigs and the others already named, strung out in a rough crescent to the south—volcanic interjections, part of that 'Ring of Fire' mentioned earlier (page 7). But the country between those milder-looking hills and the Holyhead Road has graces of its own which seem to be little explored. The old road made before Telford's time runs through it and leads past *Plas Iolyn*, a mediaeval hall, now ruinous, once the home of that Rhys who bore the victorious standard at Bosworth, and later of his grandson, Ellis Prys, the notorious informer, 'Dr. Coch', who acquired the properties of the Knights of St. John at Yspytty. Another branch of the Prys family (the name contracted from ap Rhys) lived at the house a little further along, called *Gilar*, whose Jacobean gatehouse now sheltering farm implements remains intact (Plate VII a). These two houses which are so closely related to the history of the neighbourhood lie in Denbighshire just within the eastern boundary of the Park, which now follows the course of a lane leading almost due south to Bala.

The Ffestiniog–Bala road which I said was the only public highway one would need to cross in that long mountain trail from Pentre Foelas to Dolgelley, passes between the Lesser and the Greater Arenig. The former lies immediately to the north and, though a member of the 'Ring of Fire', has little allurement. It is shaped like an inverted pie-dish and smoothly clad in heather except on the east side where it breaks rough over a shelf which holds a lake—the only feature which it really has in common with its big brother. *Arenig Fawr* (Plate XVI a), like Snowdon, is an unmistakable individual though not of such finely cut features. It is massive and bull-like, with a broad flat back and only slightly raised head, creating an impression of latent power from

[1] An eminence of the mountain shown in the geological map (p. xii) as Gylchedd.

whatever angle it is viewed. In spite of its ferocious-looking crags the ascent from either side presents no difficulty to a walker. The shorter route is from Amnodd Wen Farm on the western side; the more amusing way, from the north end of the lake; this takes you first on to the flat rump of the bull which is a remarkable platform of bare rock almost dead level.

On the summit is an ancient cairn. In 1943 an American Flying-Fortress struck the mountain just below it in the mist. Its crew of six were all killed. A tablet, locally carved, carried up the mountain single-handed and placed in position by the bailiff of the estate, tells the story, and the cairn, slightly hollowed out, holds relics of the plane.

Moel Llyfnant is a compact conical hill attached by a high ridge to the south flank of Arenig. It overlooks *Pennant Lliw*, the upper valley from which the Lliw River rushes down to the head of Bala Lake through a wild and picturesque declivity, moulded by the ancient fires of Ordovician times and strewn with fragments dislodged by the Age of Ice. Looking up this valley from the main road bridge over the river, you see a striking shape like the Rock of Gibraltar looming up a couple of miles away against the higher and more distant mountain background. It is just the sort of place to picture as the perch for a romantic castle. And if you climb up to the top of that rock you will indeed find the ruin of one—the footings and first courses of a small Norman keep and bailey, all now standing no more than shoulder-height. It is called *Castell Carn Dochan*, a place to conjure visions of the olden time! And it will help to gaze on the image of one of the knightly owners of that tower when it was complete, right up to the battlements. You will find the effigy in the little (rebuilt) parish church at *Llanuwchlyn*. It represents Ieuan ap Griffith ap Madoc ap Iorwerth, dressed in the plate armour of the fourteenth century with three wolves heads embroidered on his jupon, in token of his ancestor Ririd Flaidd (the Wolf). He died in 1373, having doubtless seen service overseas with the Black Prince. Romantic, too, is the fact that at the foot of that rock there lay a buried treasure in the shape of a gold-bearing reef. Its extraction is a more prosaic story of the nineteenth century.

The Lliw valley forms a pass into the heart of this part of the mountain region which was followed by the Romans in making the road which linked their fort at Tomen-y-mur, near Ffestiniog, with that at the head of Bala Lake, within the ramparts of which now stands the farm of *Caer Gai*.

Bala Lake has two other alternative names. To the Welsh it has always been *Llyn Tegid* while to the English of former days it was Pimblemere (Old English *pemmel*, a pebble?). Also the main river flowing in has its native name, *Dyfrdwy*, but in flowing out, its English equivalent the *Dee*.

The sources of the Thames, the Severn, and the Wye are all popular objectives for the tourist, but very few seek the far more impressive source of the historic Dee. It is certainly rough going, for there is no regular path and you cannot get within three miles of the place by car. If you follow the river up from the point where it turns into the hills near Garneddwen railway station you see before you, some way off, the wall-like barrier of *Y Dduallt*—the Black Height. It looks like a mountain which, through some primaeval cataclysm, has lost one half of itself and faces you on its riven side. Towards it you mount as you advance, the stream breaking into a series of short falls. Then you come to a wide marsh absolutely level, lying right up to the foot of the Black Height, which rises perpendicular to a crest 600 feet above. This is the source of the Dee which meets salt water below the walls of Chester. The Romans who built their great legionary fortress there (naming it Deva) regarded the river as sacred and should, according to their custom, have built a temple by its highest spring. Perhaps the ruin of it is still there sunk in the peat and moss. But the whole setting is a temple in itself.

From the south end of Y Dduallt there is quite an easy ascent to the top of the cliff from which can be seen the rugged shape of *Rhobell Fawr*, which, like the Glyders, has a double crown (2,408 and 2,313 feet) the last big hill in this group, which has now assumed the shape of the stem-end of a pear, on either side of which two deep valleys are converging on Dolgelley round the broad base of the mountain and its foothills.

In a delightful wooded recess between the mountain and those foothills is the village of *Llanfachreth* called after the Celtic missionary Machrith who founded its parish church. The latter has an approach of 19 steps under a lych-gate dedicated to the memory of George III. A road from here leads into the Vale of Ganllwyd and crosses the Mawddach to join the Ffestiniog–Dolgelley road opposite a large National Trust property in which stand the two hotels of Tyn-y-groes and Dolmelynllyn Hall (both managed by the Trust) in a finely timbered park. Near the latter is one of the most shapely waterfalls in Wales. Thomas Gray, the poet, was a connoisseur of waterfalls, and an owner of the estate in the late eighteenth century linked this *Rhaiadr Du* with Gray's memory by setting up a stone beside the lower pool graven with a verse from his Latin ode to the Deity of the Grand Chartreuse. This is on the fringe of the Rhinogs and two outliers of the same estate are the two sheepwalks (shown on M.) at the foot of Y Llethr, one containing the remote little lake of *Llyn-y-Bi*.

The remaining corner of the Range (the stem-end of the pear), is closely associated with the ancient seats of the Vaughans of Nannau and Hengwrt. Here is the long famous public footpath called the *Precipice Walk* which gives admirable prospects of the woodland, torrent and mountain scenery and, in the very pick of it (as is so often the case) is the ruin of the Cistercian Abbey of *Cymmer*. It was founded late in the twelfth century. On higher ground, a little to the north-east, is the mound of a motte castle, that can only be a little earlier in date, and must represent the residence of a local magnate who was concerned in the first gift of land to the Abbey. It now carries an eighteenth century building made by the Vaughans of Nannau.

Two old bridges cross the converging rivers of Mawddach and Wnion. That over the latter, at Dolgelley, appears to show earlier work. Its seven arches are of three different periods of construction.

THE WESTERN SIDE

A small area round Blaenau Ffestiniog is not included in the Park, the slate quarries there being still in partial activity and, although the old artillery range near Trawsfynydd has not been left out, it has only just been abandoned by the War Office (1958) and it is uncertain when the public will be admitted to the former danger zone.

The most important antiquity on the western side is the Roman fort at *Tomen-y-mur*, with its little earthwork amphitheatre (actually a cockpit?) adjoining. But the *tomen* (mound), itself, is neither Roman nor Welsh. It is a Norman motte castle believed to have been constructed by William Rufus in his campaign against Gruffydd ap Cynan in 1096. A still larger English force assembled here in 1114 in which the kings Henry I and Alexander of Scotland were present with the same object, though they failed to penetrate further into Wales. At that time the Roman road traversed by these armies must still have been in good shape. The link with Caer Gai (coming direct from Chester) has recently been traced but it is still a question whether there was another leading due south to Pennal. There is an ancient route leading in that direction (part lane, part track) to the east of the road and nearly parallel to it. Where it enters the valley of the River Gain the legends 'Llech Idris' and 'Bedd Porus' are marked on M. The former is a large pre-historic monolith. That it is associated with the same national hero as the mountain (page 94) can only be a guess.

Bedd Porus—the Grave of Porius—was, until recently, marked by an inscribed stone, now carried off to the National Museum at Cardiff. This fifth-sixth century Christian is described in his epitaph as 'Homo planus'—a plain man—which has quite a nineteenth-twentieth century ring about it.

The Berwyns, the Arans, and Cader Idris

The Park boundary takes in the town of Bala and touches the end of the Lake. It then follows the road to Llangynog over the Berwyn Hills to the highest point (1,595 feet) which happens to coincide with the ninth milestone. Here also runs the boundary between the shires of Merioneth and Montgomery which keeps the watershed, and the Park boundary turns west to follow it all the way to the sea.

The Berwyn is a delightful range of uniform but never monotonous character. Rising at the edge of the Shropshire plain, it confines the upper Dee to its course all the way to Bala Lake. Its smooth, ample flanks are roundly modelled where its many tributary streams descend from the long crest that is hardly lower at any point than 2,000 feet. Its principal heights lie along a short escarpment facing south-east just before the Park can claim them, the chief being *Moel Sych* (2,713 feet). But in those last few miles which do lie within the Park, the characteristics of the range are better seen than elsewhere, as the hills rise directly above the east side of the Lake and are open to full view from the road following the opposite bank.

From Llanuwchllyn, at the head of the Lake, a road goes up the valley of the Twrch to *Bwlch-y-Groes*—The Pass of the Cross—whence it descends to Dinas Mawddwy in the Dovey Valley. This pass is on the open mountain, and the name must recall the presence of a mediaeval cross which stood there to mark the highest point of the journey and the watershed (1,700 feet). From here the mountain barrier continues unbroken, but the road may be said to mark quite definitely the end of the Berwyn Range. Looking to your right as you ascend it, a rugged mountain appears at close quarters which is clearly of a different family—another member of the Ring of Fire, Aran Benllyn.

THE ARANS

Aran Benllyn and *Aran Fawddwy* are the names of the two eminences on this mountain. They are a mile-and-a-half apart but their difference in stature is only a matter of 69 feet. Aran Fawddwy, which reaches 2,970 feet, is the highest of the whole of the long chain reaching from the English Border to the sea which (in this western part of its extent) formed the bastion of Gwynedd, the strongest of the old Welsh states, and it has always been the dividing line between North and South Wales—the River and Estuary of the Dovey acting as a natural moat.

The names of the heights derive from the two ancient districts of Penllyn and Mawddwy whose former significance has nearly passed out of mind. These two cantrefs[1] originally belonged to the Middle Kingdom of Powys, one of whose princes was the author of the large castle mound still standing at Bala. He was dispossessed by Llewelyn the Great in 1202 who destroyed the wooden castle on the mound and annexed Penllyn to his Northern Kingdom of Gwynedd. Mawddwy remained in Powys until the Edwardian conquest, when the shire of Merioneth was created. Its head town, Dinas Mawddwy, then shared honours with Bala and Dolgelley and was made one of the new boroughs.

Approaching the Arans on the Bala–Dolgelley road, the mountain cuts a fine bold figure beyond the head of the Lake, rising from the road with well rounded slopes and folds to a sharply figured crest, for the far side is indented with a long series of precipices.

The easy way up is to take the lane near the post office at Llanuwchllyn which leads to Garth Isaf Farm (a good solid house of the time of George I, bearing the date 1724 over the front door). The mountain gate is within two fields, and you then pick your own path up the broad grass-moor and need encounter no swampy ground if you keep well up to the left.

Aran Benllyn culminates in a hump of rock startlingly interlaced with veins of white quartz. *Aran Mawddwy* is a steeple-like tor surmounted by a modern cairn and triangulation-point. You may walk along the scalloped edge of the precipice between the two summits (which is not so giddy as appears from below) and gaze over a view extending as far as the Pembrokeshire hills. The last of the Berwyns are well below and, by contrast with these ragged rocks, look well groomed, as though clad in reindeer pelts. At the foot of the crags lie two lakes, *Llyn Lliwbran* and *Llyn Dyfi*; the former sends its trickle of water to the Irish Sea, the other to St. George's Channel—it is the source of the River Dovey. But perhaps the most striking thing about the mountain is the colouring of the screes which spring from high points in all the hollows and mask the lower face with their trumpet shapes. The rock fragments are bluish in tint and mixed with a clay or mould which supports vegetation. A light green mantle of grass covers them, the blue showing through.

About two miles further west there is another high point, a dome-like eminence which can hardly be called a mountain in its own right. This is *Glasgwm* (2,557 feet). The map shows a tiny pool at the very top and a small lake in the hollow just below. It looks a fascinating place but I have never managed to get there. The system ends where Cader Idris begins, the division being only slightly marked across a high

---

[1] The *cantref* was a territorial division which could be equated with the English *hundred*. Penllyn—Head of the Lake—refers to the great one, not the small tarn at the foot of the crags.

rolling plateau by the little Clywedog River, followed by the road to Machynlleth which has climbed a hill two-and-a-half miles long from Dolgelley to reach it. At the top, by the four-cross roads, is a farm house which still keeps the name it had as a famous inn whose sign was the *Cross Foxes* (the arms of the Williams family).

CADER IDRIS

This highly individual and very impressive mountain is named after a historical person who was killed in battle on the banks of the Severn (presumably against the Saxons) about the year 630. Thus, the Park begins and ends with mountains bearing the names of national heroes— the cenotaphs of the princes Llewelyn and David in the north, the Chair of Idris in the south.[1] Like the Arans, the leading feature of this mountain is its long escarpment. But whereas that of the Arans faces outwards, with its grandeur confronting only a wilderness of sheep-walks, that of Cader Idris looks inwards over the noble Mawddach Estuary (Plate XVII a) towards the populous Barmouth–Dolgelley road, from whence it can be observed to the best possible advantage, its precipices standing clear over a fringe of low wooded hills.

The south side of Cader Idris is remarkable for the deep ravine which suddenly opens at its eastern extremity and continues throughout its whole length (about 12 miles) in a dead straight line as though one of those great giants of the Welsh fairy tale had gashed it with a knife. Its presence is due to a major crack in the earth's crust which affected the whole district between here and the other end of Bala Lake, after which it is named by geologists the *Bala fault* (page 2); the crack is responsible for both that lake and the one under Cader Idris called *Tal-y-Llyn*.

At its western end the mountain is deeply cleft by a flat-bottomed valley which, at its head, is less than a 100 feet above sea-level. This is another Pennant Valley and, like its namesake in the Hebog Range, has scenic graces which are quite outstanding, and a village whose old church is also dedicated to St. Michael and therefore bears a name identical with the other—*Llanfihangel-y-Pennant*. To the threshold-stone of a ruined cottage in this remote village there may be traced the foundation of one of the great world-wide organizations. It was from here, in the year 1800, that Mary Jones, a child of 16, who had for years saved up pennies to buy a Welsh Bible, set forth to walk barefoot

---

[1] Idris was a descendant of Meirion, a son of Cunedda, who founded the district of that name, later perpetuated in the shire of Merioneth. It was Cunedda who came down from the Scottish Border in the fifth century with his tribe of Welsh-speaking Celts and settled in North Wales, driving out overseas the Irish-speaking Celts who at that time inhabited the land.

to Bala where she had heard one could be obtained from the minister, Thomas Charles. But when she got there she found that the last had been sold. Worse still, no more were to be printed. Charles was so much moved by her story and her disappointment that he gave her his own. It was this incident which prompted Charles to make the effort which brought about the foundation of the British and Foreign Bible Society. In their office in London, Mary's Bible is preserved. In her roofless cottage a memorial has now been placed.

The two most striking things in the Pennant Valley are the conical rock on which was built one of the few castles in Wales which owed its origin to a Welsh and not an English sovereign, called *Castell-y-Bere*. The other is a natural rock, but so fantastic in appearance it looks like a wizard's castle. This is *Craig-yr-Aderyn*—the Rock of the Birds. Amongst others which visit it in the Springtime is a vast company of the weird and witch-like cormorant. It is surely an exceptional circumstance for these wholly maritime creatures to foregather for nesting six miles from the sea and perhaps indicates an unbroken tradition going back to days when the sea washed the bottom of the crags.

Castell-y-Bere, whose ruins until lately were largely concealed in the mould of a picturesque oak wood, has always been surrounded by mystery. It is believed to have been built by Llewelyn the Great and again rebuilt by Edward I who went so far as to grant a borough charter to 'Beer', a settlement all trace of which has vanished. Why, anyhow, was this site selected by the great Prince? 'Is it too fanciful' asks Mr. Hemp 'to see in the ruins of the Castle of Bere the last remains of what his ambition intended to have been the nucleus of the first capital of all Wales?'[1] Perhaps that estuary which the cormorants seem to remember brought a navigable channel much nearer to the castle in the thirteenth century. The old church of Llanfihangel was probably founded many centuries before the castle but the Norman font in it may be of that date.

The Pennant Valley is mainly watered not by its own small stream, the Cader, but the *Dysynni* River which springs in Tal-y-Llyn Lake and (contrary to expectation) leaves the long straight valley of the Bala Fault to pass into it by a cleft in the southern spur of the mountain. At the point of the river's departure from the Tal-y-Llyn Valley is the little town of Abergynolwyn whose past history is largely bound up with slate quarrying in the neighbouring hills. This is the upper terminus of the Talyllyn Railway, a narrow-gauge line (2 feet 3 inches), opened for passenger traffic in 1866 and in 1950 condemned to suffer the same fate as all the other most attractive light railways in North Wales (Plate XVII b). It was saved for the tourist by the enterprise of

[1] The Western Mail, August 22, 1925.

some young enthusiasts who with their own labours put the permanent way and the antique engines and rolling-stock into good working order. In June, 1951, the line was reopened under this new management and continues to run during the season. The lower terminus adjoins the main line station at Towyn.

WAYS UP AND OVER CADER IDRIS

The highest point (2,927 feet) is in an unusual situation where the mountain has almost been cut in two by the excavation of a huge deep hollow on either side leaving only a narrow ridge between on which the summit hut stands. In each hollow there is a lake, *Llyn Cau* on the south side, *Llyn-y-Gader* on the north, and the shortest way from Dolgelley is to make for the latter by the well-beaten trail called the *Fox's Path*. This branches off the lane leading to Dyffrydan opposite the beginning of the pool called *Llyn Gwernan*. It passes near little *Llyn-y-Gafr* and it is a pull-up from there to *Llyn-y-Gader*; but the real tug comes up the next 1,000 feet of steep scree-filled gulley.

The old pony route is much easier. This leaves the lane at Dyffrydan and goes through almost the only break in the precipitous face. From there it is about a mile-and-a-half of easy walking to the top.

On the south side of the mountain the most interesting way up, as well as the shortest, is by *Llyn Cau*—the Shut-in Lake. This aptly describes its most singular feature. As a specimen of what the glacial ice could do it is cited in text-books as one of the most perfect cirque-forms in Britain. With its arctic-alpine plant life it is now protected by the Nature Conservancy and forms part of the Cader Idris Nature Reserve.

A short distance from where the road to Tal-y-llyn branches off the main road there is a green iron gate, formerly the drive to a private house. You turn in here and have a choice of two footpaths up the steep bank through the wood. One follows the chain of waterfalls which come splashing down through thickets of rhododendron. The other keeps more to the left and, in wet weather, is recommended for the less sure-footed. Both paths reunite at the opening of the cwm. Not far from the lake itself, on the left hand, there is a way up to the crest of the hollow and on, round the brim of it to the summit.

The long ridge of the mountain with its formidable eight miles of precipice comes to a sudden end in the west and is rounded off by *Craig Cwm Llwyd* (1,790 feet) where there is a drop of several hundred feet to a wide expanse of grass moor which slopes gently towards the coast. Round this abutment winds an ancient track called *Ffordd Ddu*—the Black Road. The lane from Dolgelley to Dyffrydan (metalled as far as the mountain gate) is the earlier part of it. It leads to Towyn or (by striking off it down the Gwril Valley) to *Llwyngwril*. About a hundred yards, on the right hand side, by the highest point in the track, is the remains of a large round cairn (with a sheep-pen built out of the ruin) called *Bedd-y-Brenin*—Grave of the King. The Black Road can be reached from Arthog by a branch of it which ascends the steep brow near the waterfalls of the Arthog River. Above *Pant Philyp*, on the left hand side, is a group of standing stones, a prehistoric site of uncertain nature.

SURROUNDINGS

Bala and Dolgelley. The administrative centre of Merioneth has shifted since the creation of the shire in 1282. Harlech was at first regarded as the county town. Later, the honour was shared equally with Bala, then jointly by Bala and Dolgelley. Now, except for taking turns in the holding of the Court of Quarter Sessions, the principal county functions are conducted in Dolgelley. Here the Courts of Assize are held and it is the headquarters of the Merionethshire County Council.

Bala has always been noted for its country fairs and market, formerly held in its broad main street. An old Welsh rhyme gives an indication of the chief source of its wealth. A farmer who has lost his *dafad gorniog*—horned sheep—asks a stranger if he has seen her. He is told 'I saw her at Bala after she had sold her wool, sitting in a chair in front of a big fire, smoking a pipe and calling for a pint of beer.' But the town has not managed to preserve many buildings associated with its long history. Barclay's Bank occupies the house where Thomas Charles, the founder of the British and Foreign Bible Society, lived (page 95). He has a statue in Tegid St. *Llanycil*, a mile-and-a-half away on the lakeside (an ancient foundation but much restored), was the parish church of Bala until the present one was built in 1855. The *Lake* contains a variety of coarse fish as well as trout and a rare member of the salmon family, the *gwyniad*.

A striking feature of *Dolgelley* is the way in which its houses are built of the local hard igneous rock in large blocks, giving it a thoroughly mountain-made look. Its seven-arch bridge appears to be partly mediaeval with a variety of later constructions. The parish church, rebuilt in 1719 of dressed shale, has a roof supported on two rows of fir poles, locally grown. It contains the fourteenth century effigy of an ancestor of the Vaughans of Nannau. In the County Hall hang portraits of local nineteenth century squires.

The Coast. South of Barmouth estuary, following the fine sweep of sandy beach at Fairbourne, a range of sheer cliffs marks the foot of

Cader Idris. Curiously situated on the mountain slope above these cliffs is the old church of *Llangelynin* (the second foundation of sixth century Celynin in the Park, page 64)—severely simple with a large porch-bellcote. In it is a bier made with shafts to be borne by mountain ponies. A similar one is in *Llangower* church on the far side of Bala Lake. A little further east, overlooking the entrance to the Pennant Valley is *Llanegryn* Church which contains a perfect rood-loft and screen richly carved by a local craftsman of about the year 1500.

Between Llanegryn and Towyn, near the bridge over the Dysynni, is the castle mound, *Domen Dreiniog*, an early seat of the Princes of Gwynedd, before the great work of Castell-y-Bere, higher up the river, was built; and no doubt royal bounty is reflected in the building of the neighbouring parish church of *Towyn* with its arcades and clerestory in the late Norman manner. Since the fifth century Towyn had been an important centre of the Celtic Church (*clas*) and it possesses two inscribed stones of early date. That within the church is of special interest, as bearing the earliest inscription in Welsh known to exist (c. seventh century).

Aberdovey, the most southerly point to lie within the Park, is an ancient seaport. It still preserves the building (though much altered) which was its custom house in the early eighteenth century and was then occupied by that remarkable man, Lewis Morris, who besides being preventive officer of the port was the first to produce reliable charts of the Welsh coast for the Admiralty. He was, in addition, poet, philologist, and antiquary. The time-honoured ferry across the entrance to the Dovey estuary, which had fallen into disuse, has been restored through the energies of a local man and the iron staging built on the sandbank opposite is to signal from. This short cut brings Aberystwyth within 10 miles of the town, as against 28 by road.

The more westerly Roman road going from North to South Wales crossed the Dovey near *Pennal* between Aberdovey and Machynlleth. Cefn Gaer Farm stands on the site of the north-west angle of the fort through which the road passed (page 25) to Dolgelley and Tomen-y-mur. Little of it is to be seen above ground.

A SHORT BIBLIOGRAPHY

GENERAL

The Mountains of Snowdonia. Ed. Carr & Lister, Crosby Lockwood. The most useful all-round book about the Northern part of the Park. New ed. 1948.

Snowdonia. A symposium in the New Naturalist Library, Collins.

The Lakes of Wales. Frank Ward, Herbert Jenkins.

The World of Wales. Edmund Vale, Dent.

Snowdonia. Little Guides, Methuen.

On Foot in North Wales. Patrick Monkhouse, Maclehose. An excellent guide to the walker. It covers the whole of the Park area.

Wandering in Wales. W. A. Poucher, Country Life. Mainly excellent photographs.

Snowdonia National Forest Park Guide. H.M. Stationery Office, 1954.

Local Information-sheets giving historical, archaeological, and topographical details of particular areas and a map. Those covering the Park are Bangor, Caernarvon, Criccieth, Barmouth, Dolgelley, Machynlleth, Corwen and Bala, Conway Valley. Issued by the British Travel and Holidays Association and Crosville Motor Services Ltd., price 4d. each. Available locally at Crosville depots or their head office, Crane Wharf, Chester.

ARCHAEOLOGICAL

West of Offa's Dyke, Vol. ii. Maxwell Fraser, Hale, 1959.

The Heart of Northern Wales. W. Bezant Lowe, 2 vols. Caxton Press, Llanfairfechan. A rather amateurish compilation but containing much information not available elsewhere.

The Early Christian Monuments of Wales. V. E. Nash-Williams, University of Wales Press. A four guinea book but the most authoritative work on the subject.

Caernarvonshire vol. I (East) 1956. Royal Commission on Ancient Monuments. H.M. Stationery Office.

Segontium and the Roman Occupation of Wales. Sir Mortimer Wheeler.

Archaeologia Cambrensis.

Transactions of the Caernarvonshire Historical Society.

AUTOBIOGRAPHY

I Bought a Mountain. Thomas Firbank, Harrap.

Take not our Mountain. Dorothy Campion, Dent.

Straw into Gold. Edmund Vale, Methuen.

CLIMBING

Rock-climbing in North Wales. George and Ashley Abraham. Keswick.
Climbing in the Ogwen District. J. M. Archer Thomson, Climber's Club.
By the same author and publisher: *Lliwedd; Snowdon.*
The Climbers' Club Guide-books—*Cwm Idwal; Tryfan; Glyder Fach; Lliwedd; Llanberis Pass; The Carneddau.*
On Climbing. Charles Evans, Museum Press.
Snowdon Biography. Winthrop Young, Sutton & Noyce, Dent.

FICTION

One Green Bottle. Elizabeth Coxhead, Faber.
Death on Milestone Buttress. Glyn Carr, Geoffrey Bles.
Death under Snowdon. Glyn Carr, Geoffrey Bles.
The Offing. Edmund Vale, Dent.

LOCAL HISTORIES

History of Barmouth. E. Rosalie Jones, John Evans. Contains a good account of the gold-mining in the neighbourhood of Dolgelley.
Echoes of Old Merioneth. Hugh J. Owen, Hughes Bros., Dolgelley.
Observations on the Snowdon Mountains. William Williams of Llandegai.
A rare book. Gives an interesting account of the district in the early nineteenth century. Pub. 1802.

PLANT LIFE

'Cader Idris: a study of certain plant communities in south-west Merionethshire'. E. Price Evans. *Journal of Ecology*, vol. 20, pp. 1–52, 1932.
'Notes on the flora of Snowdonia'. J. B. Farmer, in *The Mountains of Snowdonia* by H. R. C. Carr and G. A. Lister. London: Crosby Lockwood, 1948.
The Flora of Anglesey and Carnarvonshire. J. E. Griffith, Bangor, 1895.
'The vegetation of the north-western Conway Valley, North Wales'. R. E. Hughes, *Journal of Ecology*, vol. 37, pp. 306–334, 1949.
'Plant Life' in *Snowdonia* (*National Forest Park Guide*). N. Woodhead, H.M. Stationery Office, 1954.

INDEX TO PLACES AND TOPOGRAPHICAL FEATURES

PRINCIPAL references in italic, thus '*75*'. Most of the lakes are given under 'Lyn - - '. Note on the spelling of Welsh place-names, P. 60.

(78313)   Wt. 3377   K.20   3/60   **Hw.**